Alfred (

MW00654226

50 Theses on the Expulsion of the Germans from Central and Eastern Europe 1944–1948

50 Theses on the Expulsion of the Germans from Central and Eastern Europe 1944–1948

Foreword

The initial shorter version of these Theses was published in 1986 in German as an appendix to my book, *Anmerkungen zur Vertreibung* (Kohlhammer, Stuttgart; the English language version of the book was published by Palgrave/ Macmillan under the title: *A Terrible Revenge,* but without including the theses, which are being published here for the first time in English). The original German version consisted only of twenty-two brief theses, ten historical, six on international law, and six conclusions. Upon publication they were well-received among scholars and reviewed positively by the foremost German

Professor Dr. Alfred-Maurice de Zayas

historical and educational journals *Historische Zeitschrift* and *Geschichte in Wissenschaft und Unterricht*. In fact, the theses were intended for classroom instruction in history and political science to facilitate the interdisciplinary discussion.

Much has happened since that first publication, notably the reunification of Germany, the collapse of the Soviet Union, and the implosion of Yugoslavia with the phenomenon of forced population transfers, commonly known as "ethnic cleansing". Not only have I given these events much thought over the intervening years, but I have also continued my research into the archives and exchanged views with scholars and victims of the expulsion, received many helpful suggestions from professors, political scientists, American, Polish, Czech, Russian, German and Swiss colleagues, most notably from journalist and economist Konrad Badenheuer, who has greatly contributed to the further development of the Theses. He and I have discussed all fifty back and forth, yielding both elaboration and improvement. To him I give thanks and due recognition as well as to those many colleagues and archivists who assisted me in the United States, Canada, Great Britain, Germany, Austria and Switzerland.

In 1993/94, when I was international law professor at DePaul University in Chicago, I organized an exhibition entitled "Ethnic Cleansing 1944–1948", which documented in pictures from the US Army Archives, Swiss Red Cross Archives and Bundesarchiv Koblenz, the expulsion of east European ethnic Germans. Students, professors and press visited and favourably reported on the exhibition, and I gave several lectures based on these historical and international law theses. By their nature and intent the theses presented a didactic challenge for me, since, as a teacher, I wanted to set forth the events in proper historical context and highlight their legal significance, in particular the importance of the phenomenon well beyond the specific German particulars. Of course, I realized that most of the visitors of the exhibit hardly knew anything about the historical and human rights aspects of the expulsion. My hope was that recognition of the enormity of the tragedy would be conducive to genuine reconciliation among the peoples involved and provide a lesson for the future.

The expulsion of the Germans is without question a historical event of considerable demographic, political, economic, sociological, philosophical, cultural and psychological implications, many of these only now being explored by scholars and civil society. Hundreds of masters and doctoral dissertations could be written about the multiple aspects of this human tragedy, focusing also on the sequels of the expulsion in Germany and its implications in a worldwide context, as well as on the subsequent migration of expelled Germans to the United States, Canada, Argentina, Australia, etc. Such dissertations are vitally necessary, because many gaps in this field of research must still be filled, and new perspectives can help us better understand the prodigious scale of the tragedy and its world-wide implications beyond the German experience.

At the heart of this scholarly and didactic activity lies a commitment to human dignity and to the fundamental principle of equality before the law—not just for victims, but for everyone. What is the significance of a statistic which points to around 19 million Germans and ethnic Germans who considered east-central and Eastern Europe their homelands? What is the statistical significance of 12 million such Germans expelled, four million allowed to remain in their homes but for the most part without rights or minority protection (many of these eventually emigrated to West Germany since 1950); the statistic of one million war dead and two million killed or perished in the course of the expulsion and its aftermath? Behind such cold statistics stand human faces and lives. Each and every victim demands our recognition and solidarity, above all they demand our honest effort toward rehabilitation, restitution and acknowledgement of their status as victims.

No one should accept simplistic explanations of the expulsion. No one should fall for ideological or politically-motivated paradigms. To any neutral observer it is obvious that the Second World War was the occasion but not the cause of the expulsion. The oft espoused simplistic formula of cause/effect mirrored in war/expulsion is both unconvincing and factually insupportable. Every scholar knows that *post hoc ergo propter hoc* (after the fact therefore because of it) paradigms entail a grave logical fallacy. The fact that the expulsion chronologically occurred after the Nazi crimes does not mean that it was their necessary and foreseeable consequence. An end to the Second World War without the expulsion of eastern European ethnic Germans was entirely conceivable. Actually, such an end of the war would have been required pursuant to the Atlantic Charter of August 1941. There was, however, a brutal expulsion and denial of self-determination to the east European Germans. No expulsions, however, occurred in the western provinces of Germany. It suffices to observe that the German population residing in the lands along the Rhine River were not subjected to expulsion eastward by the victorious French, Belgian or Dutch authorities, The Germans of Aachen, Düsseldorf, Krefeld, Trier remained in their homes and were not "ethnically cleansed". So why were East Prussians and Sudetenland Germans forcibly evicted, expropriated and driven to the west?

The historical cause of the expulsion from East Prussia, Pomerania and Silesia, East Brandenburg, Bohemia and Moravia, Hungary and Yugoslavia was the result of decisions made by a relatively small number of politicians representing several countries whose longstanding geopolitical agendas, jealousies and calculations resulted in the greatest forced migration of a civilian population in history. The records of the Conferences of Teheran, Malta, Yalta and Potsdam indicate that the expulsions were driven by the ambitions of Russian, Czech, Polish and Yugoslav politicians. The argument that they were a response to or reprisal for Nazi crimes was formulated much later *ex post facto* when political scientists were looking for a plausible or politically correct explanation of the unprecedented humanitarian disaster. This pseudo-explanation of the expulsion entails an instrumentalization of the collective guilt doctrine and reflects an artificial and simplistic division of the world into categories of innocent victims (Poles, Czechs, Russians) and evil perpetrators (Germans). The collective guilt thesis is, however, historically unsustainable and, beyond that, clearly incompatible with human rights norms and contrary to well established principles of due process and the rule of law. There was and is no collective guilt of the Eastern Germans for the crimes perpetrated by the Nazis and any such suggestion entails in itself a separate and distinct violation of human dignity.

As a non-German I wish to record my personal respect and sympathy for all victims, whether they be Jews, Poles, Czechs, Slovaks, Hungarians, Russians, Ukainians, Serbs, Bosnians, Croatians, Slovenians, Roma, Sinti, Germans or Austrians. I bow my head before their suffering.

All expulsions violate international law, not only according to today's norms but also according to the principles and rules of international law applicable in the years 1944 to 1948. The expulsions must not be explained away on the basis of an anachronistic and unhistorical victim/perpetrator paradigm. They must be unequivocally condemned as crimes against humanity. To this end the right to one's homeland, the security in one's home, the respect for culture and tradition must attain universal recognition. The words of the first UN High Commissioner for Human Rights, Dr José Ayala Lasso in 1995 and again in 2005, along with the concluding report of the UN Special Rapporteur on the Human Rights Dimensions of Population Transfers, Awn Shawkat Al-Khasawneh (today a judge at the International Court of Justice in The Hague), give us potent arguments for a formal codification of the right to one's homeland through the United Nations. Additionally, the Centre against Expulsions foundation in Berlin and its connection to the League of Expellees, representing the largest and most peaceful association of expellees in history, contribute to this cause as a living memorial while performing a general effort to inform the general public and to shed light on the histories of its members and to work for prevention of any such future atrocity.

It is hoped these Theses will promote a better understanding of the multiple aspects of the historical events and consequences of this "tragedy on a prodigious scale" as Churchill called it. May they contribute to the recognition of the victims *as victims*. When we consider our mutual responsibilities we are forced to the conclusion that the written histories of many nations are deliberately skewed against the victims, that prejudice and resentment work against the rehabilitation of the German expellees—yes, even after more than 66 years since war's end and the expulsion. Therefore it is welcome to see the humane overtures made to victims from the Baltic States, Hungary and Rumania. They have thus demonstrated not only a generous example of humanity and cultural tolerance but they have also in a way proved that such an enormous injustice as the expulsion of the Germans can be honorably overcome, at least in gradual steps forward, working from recognition of the causes of the expulsion to the rehabilitation of and reparation to the victims.

Professor Dr. Alfred-Maurice de Zayas

Geneva, January 2012

About the Author

Alfred-Maurice de Zayas, retired member of the New York Bar, Florida Bar, Juris Doctor (Harvard) and historian (Dr. phil. Göttingen), former Secretary of the United Nations Human Rights Committee and Chief of the Petitions Department of the UN High Commissioner for Human Rights (retired). Dr. de Zayas has been a consultant for the Office of the High Commissioner for Human Rights, frequently participates in UN panels and workshops in Geneva, and is currently Professor of International Law and World History at the Geneva School of Diplomacy. He lectures as guest professor at several universities in the United States, Canada, Ireland, Spain and Switzerland. He is the author of nine books and more than 200 scholarly articles, member of PEN International, was President of the Swiss PEN Club 2006–2009, and has been honoured for his translations of Rainer Maria Rilke and Hermann Hesse. In March 2011 at the University of Toronto he was awarded the "Educators Award" of the organization Canadians for Genocide Education.

The Theses

Historical Theses

1. The German presence in Central and Eastern Europe reaches back into the early and high middle ages. German settlement of the east was at that time predominantly a peaceful process, one which often took place with the consent or by invitation of local authorities. In a time long before the rise of modern national consciousness, large regions of Central and East Europe changed in ethnic and linguistic identity. In the late 14th Century, a hundred years before the European discovery and settlement of America, the German ethnic consolidation of Central and Eastern Europe reflected in large measure the people living there right up to the wartime flight and expulsion of the Germans in the years 1944 to 1948.

2. Only in certain regions did violence precede German settlement, namely in East Prussia, directed against the still heathen West Baltic Prussians. However, this circumstance cannot be used to justify the the expulsion of the East Prussians of the area seven hundred years after the settlement of the area. If this were somehow justifiable, then the white Europeans who migrated to and conquered North and South America, Australia and New Zealand, would have no right to remain in their homes. Indeed, the Europeans were the migrants of the 16th-20th centuries, who expanded to territories inhabited by millions of American and Australian indigenous peoples. The suggestion of some "aboriginal Slavic right" to East Prussia or Pomerania is invalid and anachronistic. Interestingly, the Nazi regime made an analogous argument by claiming that huge territories in Eastern Europe—including most of modern Poland—until the 5th century A.D. had been the homelands of Germanic tribes like the Goths, the Burgundians and the Silingen. As an example, one consequence of the Germanic presence was renaming the (in any case

German) town of Gdingen to "Gotenhafen" in 1939. The historical misconception of a violent German *Drang nach Osten* (Push to the East) is easily refuted and, in any case not representative, for in fact there was a gradual Slavic *Drang nach Westen* (Push to the West) which has been part and parcel of long-term Russian foreign policy from Peter the Great right up to Stalin.

3. The course of eastern settlement can be sketched in this way: First, the early Bavarians (Baiern) settled along the Danube eastward up to the Theiss (Tiza) River. In the 10th Century settlements of Bavarians and Franks arose in the region south of the Danube tributary Drau (Drava) River. Since the 10th Century Germans have been living in Bohemia and Moravia (Prague, Eger[1] 1061), whose rulers, as early as the 13th Century, invited German settlers: artisans, farmers and miners. In the 12th and 13th Centuries German farmers, tradesmen and monks settled in Pomerania (Stettin, incorporated pursuant to Magdeburg law *Stadtrecht* 1237/43), in the more eastern Pommerellen (German settlement of Danzig in 1178) and in Silesia (Breslau 1225). German settlement reached Posen in 1253, Cracow in 1257 and Lithuania in the 14th Century. Similarly, beginning in the 12th Century, Hungarian monarchs called for German farmers, miners and artisans to settle in the Carpathian mountains and in Transylvania (in German: *Siebenbürgen*), where they founded the town of Hermannsdorf (1192–96), destroyed by Mongols 1242/51 and rebuilt in 1366 as Hermannstadt (today Sibiu). After the invading Mongolian storms, Germans were invited by Hungarian King Bela IV to settle in Hungary, in Buchenland (Bukovina). At the same time Galicia benefited from the arrival of German settlers (Lemberg after 1300). The Teutonic Order, invited by the Duke of Masovia and authorized by the Golden Bull of Rimini (1226) of Holy Roman Emperor Frederick II of Hohenstaufen, opened up Prussian lands starting in 1230 establishing towns (Memel 1252, Königsberg 1255) and settling German farmers in the countryside[2]. In Livland and Kurland (Riga 1201, Reval 1227) middle class townsfolk and nobles arrived. Many towns and cities founded in Poland, Bohemia and Hungary were the work of Germans, or they

---

1 Eger was incorporated into Bohemia many centuries later.
2 Klaus Neitmann, *Die Staatsverträge des Deutschen Ordens in Preussen 1230–1449,* Boehlau Verlag, Cologne 1986.

were incorporated under and protected by German law. After the Turkish wars, especially in the 18th Century, a new wave of German farmers settled in the devastated and depopulated middle Danube basin. Later these people came to be called *Ungarndeutsche* (Hungarian Germans) and *Donauschwaben* (Danube Swabians). They also came to settle in present day Croatia (Slavonia) and Serbia (Voyvodina). In the 18th and 19th Centuries more Germans settled in Poland (the Weichsel Germans) and in Galicia, as well as in Dobrudscha (Dobrogea). The majority of Russian Germans, not counting those long settled there in larger cities, are descendants of farmers and peasants who, at the invitation of Catherine the Great and Alexander the First, settled along the Volga beginning in 1764, as well as in the Black Sea regions and the Caucasus. Some are descendants of German settlers in Bessarabia (1812/14, 1842) and in Volhynia (beginning 1830). During World War Two approximately 2.5 million Russian Germans were deported to Central Asian Russia, Siberia and North Russia, a fate which many of these people had already endured before, during the First World War.

4. In accordance with the 1919 treaties of Versailles, St. Germain and Trianon, around 2.4 million Germans remained within the newly established Polish state, 3.5 million German Austrians in the newly founded Czechoslovakia, 600,000 in Hungary, a further 600,000 in the newly formed Yugoslavia and 800,000 in Rumania. The civil rights of these groups were supposedly protected by treaties and further guarantees through the League of Nations Minority Rights Protections System. That system, however, was sabotaged by the governments of those countries who refused to abide by their international commitments, as documented in thousands of contemporary petitions from ethnic Germans addressed to the League of Nations in Geneva and by several judgments issued by the Permanent Court of International Justice in The Hague[3]. In Poland from 1919 until 1924 discrimination against Germans already took on the characteristics of an expulsion. In these six years

---

3 A. de Zayas, „Vertreibung und Völkerrecht": in *Flucht Vertreibung Integration*, Catalogue for the exhibition in Bonn, Berlin, Leipzig, edited by the Haus der Geschichte der Bundesrepublik Deutschland, Kerber Verlag, Bielefeld, 3rd edition 2006, pp. 180–187. A. de Zayas, *Nemesis at Potsdam*, Picton Press, Rockland, Maine; revised edition (2003), pages 4–6

alone the population of Germans in Posen, West Prussia (Pommerellen) and eastern Upper Silesia dropped by nearly one half. By 1939, on the eve of World War Two, over one million Germans had migrated from Poland to the Reich, but19 million ethnic Germans still resided east of the current Oder-Neisse border, among them some 10 million within the realm of the older Reich provinces of East and West Prussia, Pomerania, East Brandenburg, Lower Silesia, Upper Silesia as well as Danzig and Memel; 150,000 were resident in the Baltic states; 3.2 million Sudeten Germans (approximately 3 million German Bohemians and German Moravians were brought back into the Reich with incorporation of the Sudetenland enabled by the Munich Agreement of 1938); 150,000 ethnic Germans in Slovakia, 1.2 million still in Poland, nearly 600,000 in Hungary, 800,000 in Rumania, 600,000 in Yugoslavia and Bulgaria, and ca. 2.5 million in the Soviet Union.[4]

5. The flight, deportation and expulsion of ethnic Germans at the conclusion of World War Two was the greatest demographic upheaval of the 20th Century, and one of the worst in all history. Numerically speaking only the so called population exchange between Pakistan and India in the years 1947 and 1948 comes close to the expulsion of the Germans from east and southeastern Europe. As a mutual agreement between India and Pakistan and with much less bloodshed, and further without the unilateral expropriations, that exchange is only very conditionally comparable to the expulsion of Germans. Indeed the expulsion in both its breadth and lethal consequence far exceeds the "ethnic cleansing" conducted by Serbia in the former Yugoslavia between 1991 and 1999. Moreover these "cleansings" have since been rectified in part through the enforcement of the right to return and the right to restitution.[5]

---

4 Gerhard Reichling, *Die deutschen Vertriebenen in Zahlen*, Bonn, 1986. A. de Zayas, *Nemesis at Potsdam*, table on page XXV, *A Terrible Revenge*, pp. 155–156
5 The legal basis was provided by the Dayton Accords of December 14, 1995 as well as many resolutions of the UN Security Council and General Assembly concerning the right of return and restitution, as implemented in relevant judgments of the Human Rights Chamber in Sarajevo. See A. de Zayas, "The Right to One's Homeland, Ethnic Cleansing and the International Criminal Tribunal for the Former Yugoslavia" in *Criminal Law Forum*, Vol. 6, pp. 257–314. *Human Rights Chamber for Bosnia and Herzegovina, Digest of Decisions on Admissibility and Merits 1996–2002.* N. P. Engel, Kehl 2003.

6. The term "expulsion" can be justifiably applied not only to the wild evictions and pogroms of 1945, but also to the subsequent "population transfers" of 1946–1948. Moreover, the organized evacuations conducted by German authorities beginning in the autumn of 1944 and the massive flight in the spring of 1945 became part of the general expulsion, owing to the fact that those evacuated and those who fled were later denied the right to return to their homes and property. The use of the term "expulsion" as regards these unfortunate civilians is proper, in that they were forced to lose not only their homeland but all their possessions as well. The hard fact of the expulsion cannot be diminished by use of euphemisms such as "displacement", "resettlement", "migration", "emigration" or even "enforced emigration".[6] The recently coined euphemism "ethnic cleansing" is objectionable for a number of reasons, as it would appear to white-wash a crime against humanity by associating it with the idea of "cleansing" a territory, as if the indigenous population of East Prussia or Pomerania had somehow defiled the territory by their presence. Nevertheless, to the extent that the "ethnic cleansing" practiced in the former Yugoslavia has been recognized by the United Nations as a form of genocide, the term could be applied by analogy to the expulsion of the Germans, which was greater in scope and more costly in terms of human lives.

7. World War Two delivered a convenient opportunity to expel millions of human beings from their homelands, but it was neither its cause nor a justification. The true causes of this unprecedented event were deliberate decisions taken by politicians who each had geopolitical and economic interests and agendas. The records of the Conferences of Teheran, Malta, Yalta and Potsdam, countless memoranda of the US State Department and British Foreign Office, proclamations by politicians and other documents, particularly the revealing statements by Czech, Polish, Yugoslav and Soviet politicians prove the point. The larger causes of the expulsion were specifically connected to the geopolitical ambitions of Stalin and the desire of

---

6 Manfred Kittel, *Vertreibung der Vertriebenen? Der historische deutsche Osten in der Errinnerungskultur der Bundesrepublik.* Series of the Vierteljahrshefte für Zeitgeschichte, Oldenbourg Verlag, Munich 2007, p. 164. Matthias Stickler, *Ostdeutsch heißt Gesamtdeutsch*, Droste Verlag, Düsseldorf, 2004, p.124.

the Western Allies to weaken Germany permanently. Similar endeavors on the part of Czech and Polish politicians can be documentarily traced back several decades before the Second World War and Hitler's ascension to power.[7] Consequently the expulsions cannot be viewed simplistically from the perspective of September 1, 1939, Hitler's invasion of Poland. The causes of the expulsion must be sought as well in the dynamic Slavic nationalism arising in the 19th Century along with resolutions made in the 1919 treaties of Versailles, St. Germain and Trianon. The expulsion was not punishment for Auschwitz and at no point in the deliberations at Teheran, Yalta or Potsdam did the Allies formulate a causal nexus between the Nazi persecution of Jews and gypsies and the expulsion of the Eastern Germans. To pretend that Hitler was the cause of the expulsion is simplistic and unhistorical. Post hoc ergo propter hoc remains a fallacy of logic.

8. After the subjugation of Poland in September, 1939, both Hitler and Stalin employed similar methods to perpetuate domination over their respective shares of the booty. Hitler annexed regions in western Poland that had been lost to Germany as a consequence of the Versailles Treaty, deporting around 920,000 Poles farther east to the so-called General Gouvernement under German occupation. In connection with this move, various German ethnic groups, namely Baltic and Bessarabian Germans released from the Soviet sphere of influence, were brought to those western regions as part of the Nazi "Home to the Reich" (Heim ins Reich) policy[8]. Meanwhile Stalin looked to strengthen his hold on the lands east of the so-called Ribbentrop-Molotov Line by deporting anti-soviet Poles and murdering the Polish military elite (Katyn massacre, Spring 1940). After the start of the eastern campaign of June 1941, Hitler planned on large German settlement complexes in the European parts of the Soviet Union and would

7 See among others Carl Jacob Burckhardt, *Meine Danziger Mission* 1937–1939, Munich 1960, 3rd expanded edition 1980, p. 156f. Roland Gehrke, *Der polnische Westgedanke bis zur Wiedererrichtung des polnischen Staates nach Ende des Ersten Weltkrieges,* Marburg 2001. Fritz Peter Habel, *Dokumente zur Sudetenfrage*, 5th edition, Munich 2003, p. 240f. Viktor Burns, *Die Tschechoslowakei auf der Pariser Friedenskonferenz, in: Zeitschrift für ausländisches öffentliches Recht und Völkerrecht* vol. VIII (1938), pp. 607–623.
8 Alfred de Zayas "International Law and Mass Population Transfers" *Harvard International Law Journal* (1975) pp. 201–258.

have forcibly resettled many Russians and Ukrainians if he had won the war (General Plan East).[9]

9. The principle of forced resettlement was first proposed in the West by Czech political exile Eduard Beneš. His "offer" dated September 15, 1938 would cede approximately 18% of the Sudetenland to Germany provided that some 55% of the Sudeten Germans left the country—a barely disguised expulsion plan. Soon after the Munich Agreement of September 30, 1938 and before the outbreak of the war, in talks with Stalin, Churchill and Roosevelt, Beneš was already pressing anew for the "transfer" of the largest possible number of Germans out of Czechoslovakia. Initially a few hundred thousand Sudeten Germans were to be affected who had—according to Beneš—proved disloyal to the Czechoslovakian state, and that they furthermore were active as a fifth column in the service of Hitler. Later, in talks with the Allies, Beneš openly pursued a total Sudeten German expulsion and confiscation of their property as his primary war aim. Beneš thereby abandoned any principle of responsibility or guilt. The goal was—analogous to the ideology of German National Socialism—a nationally homogenous, purely Slavic Czechoslovakian state cleansed of any German or Hungarian minorities, as illustrated in Beneš Decrees 12, 33 and 108.

10. After the principle of the forced resettlement of the supposedly disloyal Sudeten German minority had been accepted by the Allies, the process was extended to the Germans residing in the eastern provinces of the Reich where they constituted the centuries-old indigenous population and were not at all a minority. At the Teheran Conference (November 28 to December 1, 1943) Stalin's demand to annex Polish territory east of the Ribbentrop-Molotov Line led to a decision that this annexation be accomplished at the expense of German provinces in the west. At first glance this exchange might seem equitable, yet by the same token it is ethically and legally inacceptable since the territories governed by Poland from 1919/20 until 1939 east of the Curzon Line (majority Ukrainian, White Russian and

---

[9] Wolfgang Benz, „Der Generalplan Ost" in: W. Benz, *Die Vertreibung der Deutschen aus dem Osten*, 2nd edition, Berlin 1995, pp. 45–47.

partially Lithuanian settlements won by Poland in a war of aggression against Russia in 1920) held roughly 2.5 million Poles, while in the pre-war Polish regions alone more than two million Germans had lived for generations. Stalin sought a geopolitical upheaval with a Soviet and Polish expansion westward. And finally, German territories were to be rid of all German populations. As the documents from the Teheran, Yalta and Potsdam Conferences confirm, neither the Nazis' forced resettlements in the East nor other Nazi crimes played a role in the decision to expel the Germans from eastern Germany. The assertion that there existed a cause-and-effect nexus between the Nazi General Plan East (*Generalplan Ost*) and the expulsions is a *red herring*, factually and historically unsustainable.

11. The pertinent records in London's Public Record Office and in the National Archives in Washington D.C. show that experts in the Foreign Office and the State Department—until the Conferences of Malta, Yalta and Potsdam—held out for limits on the territorial compensation to Poland and its attendant "resettlement" of ethnic Germans on grounds that it violated international law. At first only East Prussia, Danzig and parts of Upper Silesia, then maximally some additional territory to the Oder River, a not insignificant part of Silesia, were to be conceded to Poland as compensaton. Moreover the whole process was to be supervised by a so-called Population Transfers Commission in order to guarantee a gradual and orderly process as well as compensation for property left behind. Diplomats justified this action with reference to the precedent of the population "exchange" that had taken place between Greece and Turkey in the years 1921–23, during the genocidal Kemalist war against the Greeks of Pontus and Ionia, and completed 1923 to 1926 pursuant to the July 1923 Treaty of Lausanne, implemented partially under the supervision of the League of Nations. However, in the case of the Germans there was no "exchange" but rather a completely one-sided expulsion into war torn landscapes which were devastated and barren, with an agriculture unable to provision the native inhabitants. Thus the Allies ended up having to confront the very real danger of mass starvation in post-war occupied Germany and to import millions of tons of grain to prevent it.

12. At the Potsdam Conference held from July 17 to August 2, 1945, the notorious Article XIII of the Communiqué reflects the Allies' deliberations on the issue of the "transfer" of Germans.[10] This article was and continues to be misinterpreted especially when it is claimed that the Anglo-Americans had advocated or even agreed to the final, actual extent of the "resettlement". This is demonstrably incorrect: Article XIII was an emergency measure that had to be put into effect in great haste because the brutal expulsions—unauthorized by the western Allies—taking place in Czechoslovakia, Poland and the eastern provinces of Germany were creating a situation of chaos in the American and British Zones, not least in Berlin, as documented in numerous American and British reports from this period. Article XIII was not a blank check for the Czechoslovakian, Polish and Hungarian authorities. In fact its goal was first to impose a moratorium on expulsions and to confer responsibility for the extent and time of further "transfers" onto the Allied Control Council in Berlin.[11] Furthermore, the Allies had not concluded a single agreement concerning the property left behind by the Germans, nor any regarding future drawing of borders. In this connection Article VI of the Potsdam Communiqué contains a reference to a future peace conference where the western Allies would support a claim on Königsberg made by the USSR. But a corresponding reference to the effect that Great Britain and the USA would support Polish claims on German territories east of the Oder-Neisse line was deliberately left out. Article IX of the Communiqué stipulates that the territories would be given over to Polish *administration* only, indicating that the USA and Great Britain, likewise with respect to the expulsions, wanted to revisit the issue in the light of a post-war European peace settlement. The fact that 45 years later, in 1990, the Oder-Neisse Line eventually became the definitive Oder-Neisse border has nothing to do with the will of the British, French or American Governments in 1945 (or for that matter in 1990), but reflects the

---

10 In this Article the principle of "transfers" in an "orderly and humane" manner was recognized, indeed it even incorporated a moratorium on expulsions, with responsibility for implementation of the transfer, the number of affected persons and scheduling, resting on the Allied Control Council in Berlin. See A. de Zayas, *Nemesis at Potsdam*, Chapter V

11 See letter from Sir Geoffrey Harrison, author of Article XIII, to Sir John Troutbeck, Chief of Germany Department in the Foreign Office, dated August 1, 1945, Public Record Office, FO 371/468II, Doc. Nr. C4415, reproduced in A. de Zayas, *Nemesis at Potsdam*, facsimile in the Appendix, on pp. 232–234 and pp. 62–64 of this book.

power equation in 1945, i.e. the *fait accompli* imposed by Stalin at Potsdam, and the fact that the Soviet Union rejected all Western attempts at negotiation. With the passage of time the provisional administration matured into annexation pursuant to the dubious principle "might is right".

13.
The American and British governments protested in Warsaw and Prague against the inhumane treatment of German minorities and the non-observance of guidelines set forth in Article XIII of the Potsdam Communiqué. Unfortunately, the words were not backed up by action and remained mere diplomatic notes of protest. The deportations which followed the Allied Control Council's establishment of a reception/immigration plan in November, 1945, were carried out with fewer losses. However, in March 1950 the Walter Commission of the U.S. House of Representatives in its detailed report on the expulsion of the Germans concluded that no phase of the expulsion could be considered humane.[12] The assertion that the expulsions were conducted in "an orderly and humane manner" has since been utterly discredited by virtue of tens of thousands of individual testimonies on record in the Eastern Documentation of the German Federal Archives as well as reports made by American and British observers and diplomats in the years 1945 to 1948.[13] Since 1989 related documents have been released from Russian, Polish, Czech and Serbian archives all underscoring the brutalities suffered by the expellees.

14.
An even worse fate than that endured by the refugees and expellees befell nearly two million deportees. Here too the responsibility of the Anglo-American alliance is well documented. At the Yalta Conference on 11 February 1945, Stalin, Churchill and Roosevelt signed an agreement establishing the concept of "reparations in kind" and defining that term to encompass the use of "German labour". This common resolution with Stalin formally authorized the deportation of almost two million ethnic Germans primarily

---

12 United States House of Representatives, Report of a Special Subcommittee of the Committee on the Judiciary, pursuant to House Resolution 238, Report No. 1841, Washington D. C., March 24, 1950.
13 Th. Schieder, Hans Rothfels (Eds.): *Dokumentation der Vertreibung der Deutschen aus dem Osten,* Vols. 1–8, Part One, dtv Munich, 1984.

from Rumania, Yugoslavia and Hungary, but also from the Reich, including from East Prussia, Pomerania and Silesia—men and women—for purposes of forced slave labour in the Soviet Union as a kind of "living reparations".[14]

15. Flight, expulsion and deportation cost over two million people their lives, according to the 1958 investigation conducted and published by the German Federal Statistical Office in Wiesbaden as commissioned by the German parliament.[15] Although expulsions and deportations occurred mainly after war's end, these events were portrayed by the Allies as some sort of "peace measure". Such events must be termed crimes against humanity and the victims must be rehabilitated. When evaluating the expulsion, the 1950 Charter of the German Expellees must be taken into account. It demanded the respect of the right to one's homeland and it also pledged non-violence in achieving it.[16]

16. Since 1949, following the mass expulsions, 4.5 million German emigrants came to the West. These emigrants are in a certain sense also expellees since the same circumstances which led to expulsion have decades later made it difficult for German ethnic minorities to live as Germans in their ancestral homelands. According to UN documents, the simplest minority rights in east central and eastern Europe were systematically denied, including the right to one's own culture and language.[17] The few ethnic Germans who

---

14 . A. de Zayas, *A Terrible Revenge*, p. 85. Gerhard Reichling, *Die deutschen Vertriebenen in Zahlen*, Part 1, Table 5, p. 33.
15 German Federal Statistical Office, *Die deutschen Vertreibungsverluste*, Wiesbaden 1958. Attempts to revise down the number of eastern Germans who perished as a result of flight, expulsion and deportation are methodically flawed and intellectually unconvincing, see pp. 55–58 of this book. It should also be remembered that numbers much higher than two million deaths can be cited. In his Memoirs Konrad Adenauer noted: „I must first of all speak of the problem of expulsion. According to American figures a total of 13.3 million Germans were expelled from the Eastern part of Germany, from Poland, Czechoslovakia, Hungary, and so on. 7.3 million arrived in the Eastern zone and the three Western zones, most of these in the latter. *Six million Germans have vanished from the earth. They are dead, gone.* Most of the 7.3 million who stayed alive are women, children, and old people." Konrad Adenauer. *Memoirs, 1945–1953* (Chicago: Regnery, 1966), pp. 148–149 (emphasis supplied).
16 Alfred de Zayas, *Heimatrecht ist Menschenrecht*, Universitas, München 2001.
17 A noteworthy exception is Rumania where even during the Cold War schools with German language instruction existed, thus there was no assimilation. To be sure there was political suppression and economic misery to such a degree that from 1975 until 1990 almost 90% of Rumanian Germans left their homeland.

remained in their homelands were unable to preserve their German identity after the expulsion of their compatriots. Germans living in Czechoslovakia who had not been expelled suffered confiscation of all their property.

17. The idea that expulsions are irreversible is widespread, but not correct. In Europe and the northern Caucasus there have since been numerous examples of just the opposite. After the Second World War the deported Warthegau Poles were able to return to their homeland, so too the deported Alsatian-French. Since 1989 some 300,000 Crimean Tatars have been able to return to the Crimea, after the mass deportation in 1944. The Yugoslav upheavals of the 1990's were also followed by the return of most Bosnians and Kosovars to their homes and property. Within modern Poland there is a certain process for the right of return given to expelled Ukrainians and White Russians. This situation is cause for some hope to those peoples still disenfranchised, such as Greeks, Cypriots, Karelians, Poles from the Lviv and Vilnius

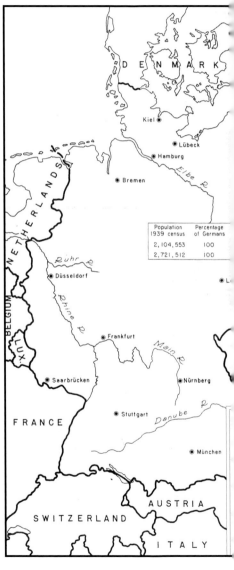

Germany and Poland: Proposed Territorial Changes (U.S. Department of State, January 10, 1945; Original Classification "Secret")

region, Chaldeo-Assyrians, Armenians, Italians from Istria, Kurds as well as
Germans from the Eastern Provinces and the Sudetenland.

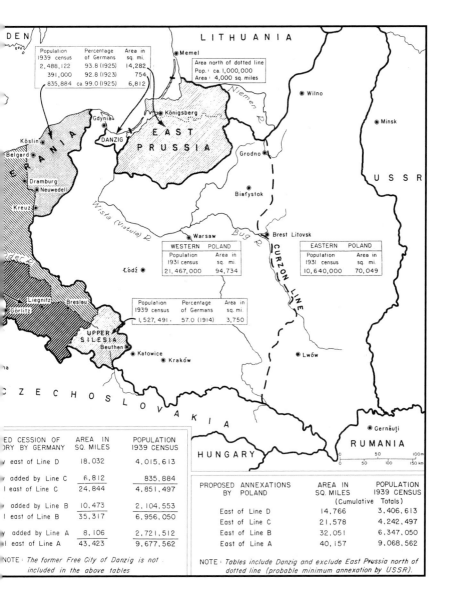

Population 1939 census	Percentage of Germans	Area in sq. mi.
2,488,122	93.8 (1925)	14,282
391,000	92.8 (1923)	754
835,884	ca. 99.0 (1925)	6,812

Area north of dotted line
Pop.: ca. 1,000,000
Area: 4,000 sq. miles

WESTERN	POLAND
Population 1931 census	Area in sq. mi.
21,467,000	94,734

EASTERN	POLAND
Population 1931 census	Area in sq. mi.
10,640,000	70,049

Population 1939 census	Percentage of Germans	Area in sq. mi.
1,527,491	57.0 (1914)	3,750

...ED CESSION OF ...RY BY GERMANY	AREA IN SQ. MILES	POPULATION 1939 CENSUS
...y east of Line D	18,032	4,015,613
...y added by Line C	6,812	835,884
...l east of Line C	24,844	4,851,497
...y added by Line B	10,473	2,104,553
...l east of Line B	35,317	6,956,050
...y added by Line A	8,106	2,721,512
...l east of Line A	43,423	9,677,562

NOTE: *The former Free City of Danzig is not included in the above tables*

PROPOSED ANNEXATIONS BY POLAND	AREA IN SQ. MILES (Cumulative Totals)	POPULATION 1939 CENSUS
East of Line D	14,766	3,406,613
East of Line C	21,578	4,242,497
East of Line B	32,051	6,347,050
East of Line A	40,157	9,068,562

NOTE: *Tables include Danzig and exclude East Prussia north of dotted line (probable minimum annexation by USSR).*

International Law Theses

18. The right to one's homeland is a human right.[18] The right to national self determination, today recognized as *jus cogens* (peremptory international law), of necessity must embrace the right to one's homeland, for self determination cannot be exercised if one is driven from one's homeland. Moreover the right to one's homeland is a precondition to the exercise of most civil, political, economic, social and cultural rights.[19] The Germans of Bohemia and Moravia (frequently referred to as Sudeten Germans) whose ancestors had resided there for seven centuries, were denied self-determination in 1919 notwithstanding their repeated appeals to the Paris Peace Conference, and notwithstanding the recommendations of the American expert, Harvard Professor Archibald Cary Coolidge, who at Paris proposed giving the territories in question to Germany and Austria in 1919. Whereas the Treaties of Versailles, St. Germain and Trianon promoted the self-determination of Poles, Czechs and Slovaks, this was done at the expense of denying self-determination to Germans and Magyars. Judged by today's standards, their claim to self-determination was equal if not superior to that of Kosovars, Transnistrians, Abkhazians, Southern Ossetians, Sudanese and many others.

19. Although the right to national self determination was not yet part of peremptory international law in 1945, the expulsions were illegal by standards of the then applicable norms of international law, and the treatment of the expelled Germans entailed war crimes and crimes against humanity.

---

18 Otto Kimminich, *Das Recht auf die Heimat*, 3rd edition, Bonn 1989 and *Die Menschenrechte in der Friedensregelung nach dem zweiten Weltkrieg*, Berlin 1990. Alfred de Zayas, *Heimatrecht ist Menschenrecht*, Munich 2001.

19 On August 6, 2005 the former UN High Commissioner for Human Rights, Dr. José Ayala Lasso, said in Berlin: "… the right to one's homeland is not merely a collective right, but it is also an individual right and a precondition for the exercise of many civil, political, economic, social and cultural rights." See A. de Zayas, *Die Nemesis von Potsdam* pp. 404–406 and p. 43 of this book.

The Hague Regulations on Land Warfare appended to Hague Convention IV of 1907 were applicable during World War Two. Articles 42–56 limit the powers of occupying nations and guarantee protection to resident populations, especially the honor and rights of the family, the lives of ordinary citizens and private property (Article 46). Collective punishments are forbidden (Article 50). Thus, any mass expulsion implies a major violation of The Hague Regulations. Moreover, pursuant to the Martens Clause[20] which formulated minimal standards of warfare as early as 1899, "cases not included in the Regulations" would necessarily have to be judged in the light of the "laws of humanity", which means that expulsions of civilians, accompanied by mass killings and complete expropriation of property would undoubtedly be illegal.[21] This Clause was then—as the later Nuremberg War Crimes Tribunals proved—a compulsory principle of international law. Therefore, those responsible for the expulsion of the Germans cannot invoke the then absence of specific international law on population transfers in order to justify the expulsion. In his *Ethics* Baruch Spinoza observed that "nature abhors a vacuum". International lawyers agree that there cannot be a "legal black hole" when it comes to the over-arching principles of human rights law. Up until December 9, 1948 international law did not stipulate a specific and explicit ban of genocide. Yet nothing could make the Holocaust compatible with international law, even in the absence of a positive norm of black letter law.

20. The expulsions cannot be interpreted as reprisals, for wartime reprisals can be undertaken only under very narrow and well defined conditions subject to principles of proportionality that underlie the international legal order. These conditions were not met at the time of the earlier expulsions of ethnic Germans up until May 8, 1945. However, the bulk of the

20 This particular achievement in international law, later cited in several international conventions as well as judgments by international courts, was conceived by the Russian Diplomat of German-Estonian heritage, an international legal authority, Friedrich Fromhold Martens (1845–1909).
21 The Martens Clause stipulates: "Until a more complete code of the laws of war has been issued, the High Contracting Parties deem it expedient to declare that, in cases not included in the Regulations adopted by them, the inhabitants and the belligerents remain under the protection and the rule of the principles of the law of nations, as they result from the usages established among civilized peoples, from the laws of humanity, and the dictates of the public conscience."

expulsion took place after the end of the war, making the legal concept of reprisal *a priori* inapplicable to this event. – The expulsions furthermore violated customary international law as well as treaty obligations protecting minority rights assumed by Poland, Czechoslovakia, Hungary and Yugoslavia in 1919. The denial of the right to return of German war refugees similarly constituted violations of international law applicable in 1945.

21. The verdict of the International Military Tribunal at Nuremberg rightly condemned the expulsions perpetrated by the Nazis against Poles mainly from the Posen and Pommerellen ("Westpreußen") regions and Frenchmen from the Alsace as war crimes and crimes against humanity. International law has *per definitionem* universal applicability, and therefore the expulsions of ethnic Germans by Poland, Czechoslovakia, Hungary and Yugoslavia, measured against the same standard, similarly constitute war crimes and crimes against humanity.[22] The harsh judgments against those German officials who ordered expulsions illustrate the international law rejection of impunity and the necessity to vindicate the principle of individual responsibility for war crimes. Moreover it should be remembered that those who had been expelled by the German Nazis were, after 1945, granted the right of return to home and property.

22. The Potsdam Conference did not conclude with an international legal accord, but solely with a final communiqué. Article XIII of the Potsdam Communiqué could not have legalized the expulsion of the Germans, even if the Agreement had been a formal treaty under international law. For no victory, even a victory by the initial victims of a war of aggression, grants unlimited powers over the lives and other elementary rights of the vanquished. Even if an Inter-Allied Transfer Accord had existed (Article XIII does not constitute such an accord) it could not have stepped over the boundaries of international law, since a treaty that violates a peremptory principle of international law such as the right to self-determination is *ab initio* invalid (Vienna Convention on the Law of Treaties, Articles 53 and 64). Yet, the history of

---

[22] In his Memoirs, Konrad Adenauer writes: "Misdeeds have been committed loathsome enough to stand alongside those committed by the German National Socialists."

humanity is filled with laws and treaties which support, codify or strengthen injustice. Mere normative formulation does not and cannot make injustice into justice, cannot confer legal status to a criminal act. Indeed, in a very real sense, under certain conditions a positivist norm can in itself constitute a crime against humanity.

23. Present day international law explicitly regards forced resettlements as criminal. Article 49 of Geneva Convention IV of August 12, 1949, respecting the protection of civilians in time of war, explicitly forbids forced resettlement. Article 17 of the Second Protocol of 1977 expressly prohibits expulsions even in local, sovereign domestic matters. In peacetime, expulsions violate the UN Charter, the Universal Declaration of Human Rights of December 10, 1948, the Human Rights Covenants of 1966 and the International Convention on the Elimination of All Forms of Racial Discrimination. Likewise they breach the Fourth Protocol to the European Convention for the Protection of Human Rights and Fundamental Freedoms, Article 3 of which reads: "1) No one shall be expelled, by means either of an individual or of a collective measure, from the territory of the State of which he is a national. 2) No one shall be deprived of the right to enter the territory of the state of which he is a national"; and Article 4 which stipulates "collective expulsions of aliens is prohibited". In war and peace expulsion and deportation represent crimes within the purview of international law. In accordance with Article 8 of the Statute of the International Criminal Court of 1998 expulsions constitute war crimes, and according to Article 7 they constitute crimes against humanity. Under certain circumstances they can also amount to genocide pursuant to Article 6.

24. Depending on intent and gravity, expulsion and deportation can qualify as genocide. According to Article II of The UN Convention on the Prevention and Punishment of the Crime of Genocide dated December 9, 1948, genocide is defined by acts or actions intended to partially or entirely destroy a certain national, ethnic, racial or religious group, primarily by killing members of these groups, or by imposing unendurable living conditions or by committing similar offenses which frequently accompany every expulsion.

Given the "intent to destroy a national, ethnic, racial or religious group" also the mental and spiritual stress accompanying mass expulsions can complete the legal conditions necessary to constitute genocide.

25. This intention to wipe out specific populations was beyond doubt the goal of both Edvard Beneš in Czechoslovakia and Josip Broz Tito in Yugoslavia, a fact sufficiently documented in their speeches and decrees. This mental prerequisite qualifies the violent expulsion of Germans from these countries as genocide. This opinion is strongly supported by prominent professors of international law including Felix Ermacora and Dieter Blumenwitz.[23] The genocidal character of the expulsions is underscored by the racial targeting of the victims, independent of any personal guilt or responsibility. Indeed, the ethnic Germans were expelled on the basis of their ethnic origin and not because of their personal conduct. As a consequence, there is an obligation for everyone (*"erga omes"*) not to recognize the consequences of the expulsion. The pseudo-principle of the "normative power of facts" is inapplicable in cases of genocide or crimes against humanity. Here the general principle of law (ICJ Statute, article 38) *ex injuria non oritur jus* (out of a violation of law no right can emerge) takes precedence.

26. The General Assembly of the United Nations, in its resolution 47/121 of December 18, 1992, categorized "ethnic cleansing", which was then taking place in Yugoslavia, as genocide. This resolution was confirmed and strengthened by many subsequent resolutions.[24] In 2001 the International Criminal Tribunal for the former Yugoslavia categorized certain acts of "ethnic cleansing" in the former Yugoslavia as genocide, namely the massacre at Srebrenica in 1995. In its judgment in the case of *Bosnia and Herzegovina vs. Federal Republic of Yugoslavia* of February 26, 2007, the International Court of Justice confirmed that the massacre of Srebrenica constituted genocide. On the basis of this judgment it can be asserted that the

---

[23] Dieter Blumenwitz, *Rechtsgutachten über die Verbrechen an den Deustchen in Jugoslawien 1944–1948*, Munich 202. Felix Ermacora, *Die Sudetendeutschen Fragen. Rechtsgutachten.* Munich 1992.

[24] GA Resolutions Nos. 48/143 of December 1993, 49/205 of December 1994, 40/192 of December 1995, 51/115 of March 1997, etc.

expulsion of the Germans, accompanied by hundreds of thousands of murders and rapes, necessarily constituted genocide, since the Russian, Polish, Czechoslovak, Hungarian and Yugoslav politicians and military commanders manifested their intent to destroy, "in whole or in part", the German ethnic group "as such". Moreover, the manner of implementation of the "population transfer" was considerably more severe and inflicted more casualties than the recent events in the former Yugoslavia. Certainly the killings that accompanied the Brünn Death March, the massacres at Nemmersdorf, Metgethen, Allenstein, Marienburg, Saaz, Postelberg, Aussig, Prerau, Filipova and at several thousand other places in addition to the massive number of deaths in the camps at Lamsdorf, Swientochlowice, Theresienstadt, Gakovo[25], Rudolfsgnad and in several hundred other camps constituted crimes against humanity and were manifestations of genocidal intent.

27. Since the late 1990s the United Nations has recognized and promoted the right to truth[26], which entails the right to historical memory. All victims of violations of human rights have a right to the truth, to their history and to recognition of their status as victims. This is a right they should insist upon. Crimes concealed by silence or untruths are more likely to be repeated, just as frivolous accusations of criminal wrongdoing violate the rights, dignity, honor and reputation of the accused (Article 17 of the UN Covenant on Civil and Political Rights).

28. International law applies equally to all peoples and states. Therefore members of the international community are *erga omnes* (in relation to everyone) obligated to uphold the norms of international law without any arbitrary exceptions. A state endangers the security of the law and puts into question the credibility of the international legal order when it applies

---

25 Detailed documentation on Gakovo is given on www.donauschwaben-usa.org, including reports of survivors like Hans Kopp.
26 On April 20, 2005 the pertinent Resolution was adopted by the UN Commission on Human Rights, Resolution 2005/66, UN Doc. E/CN.4/2005/66. See also Yasmin Naqvi, "The right to the truth in international law; fact or fiction?" *International Review of the Red Cross*, Vol. 88, June 2006, pp. 245–273. See the Report of the UN High Commissioner for Human Rights, Navi Pillay, 21 August 2009 http://www2.ohchr.org/english/bodies/hrcouncil/docs/12session/A-HRC-12–19.pdf

different standards or engages in selectivity. Genocide and crimes against humanity are equally reprehensible in all situations and they require moral rehabilitation and material reparation to all victims regardless of nationality or ethnic origin.

29. Expulsions violate not only the rights of the expellees but also the rights of the receiving host population.[27] Larger expulsions create interim shortages of essential resources, above all food and habitat. This was actually the case for Germany as the country reached a famine crisis point during the winters of 1945/46 and 1946/47, conditions that drove Germany to a veritable humanitarian catastrophe.[28] Ten thousands of deaths among the resident German population were tabulated as a result of the expulsion. However, in the middle and long run the host population profited from the mass influx of expellees while the expellees themselves had to wait a much longer time for an end of their hardship.[29]

30. According to the principle of *ubi jus, ibi remedium* (if there is law, there is a remedy) refugees and expellees are entitled to rehabilitation and restitution. They have the right to return to their homes and to the restitution of their property.[30] The Dayton Accords of 1995 drawn up to end the war in Bosnia and Herzegovina recognized these rights. Since then they have been partially realized through the activity of the Human Rights Chamber in Sarajevo. When private property is confiscated in conjunction with a crime against humanity or genocide, the state whose citizens are the victims must

---

[27] Report by the Special Rapporteur Awn Shawkat Al Kasawneh on the illegality of expulsions. UN Doc. E/CN.4/Sub.2/1997/23

[28] Victor Gollancz, *Our Threatened Values*, London 1946; Gollancz, *In Darkest Germany*, London 1947.

[29] This inter-relationship was first described and explained in its economics by Konrad Badenheuer, cf. *Die Sudetendeutschen – eine Volksgruppe in Europa*, edited by Sudetendeutscher Rat, Munich 2007, p. 98f. See also Alfred de Zayas "Marshall Plan" in Oxford Encyclopedia of Public International Law, 2010

[30] See UN Sub-commission for Human Rights, Resolutions 2002/30 and 2005/21, Final Report of the Sub-commission on the Human Rights Dimensions of Population Transfers, UN Doc. E/CN.4/Sub.2/1997/23 and the statements made by the first UN High Commissioner for Human Rights Dr José Ayala Lasso made on May 28, 1995 in Frankfurt and 2005 in Berlin. International Commission of Jurists, *The Right to a Remedy and to Reparation for gross Human Rights Violations*, Geneva 2006. See also the UN Restitutions Principles: Pinheiro Principles on Restitution http://domino.un.org/pdfs/ocha_pinheiro_principles.pdf.

step up to demand restitution through return or compensation if the offending state will not satisfy these demands through its own legal apparatus. It is not a question of diplomatic discretion whether or not to press the claims of the victims, it is a matter of an *erga omnes* obligation to reverse the effects of crimes against humanity and genocide and to vindicate the primacy of law over politics.[31]

31. All victims of expulsion have a right to compensation and no statute of limitations applies, precisely because expulsion is a grave violation of human rights in the category of crimes against humanity. While a victim in pursuit of his legal rights cannot apply to the International Court of Justice in The Hague (only sovereign nations may do so), application can be made to the European Court of Human Rights or to the United Nations Human Rights Committee after first having recourse to and exhausting domestic remedies. Victims should in general insist on their rights, not for material advantage but in order to strengthen the rule of law and the credibility and legitimacy of international law. The right to the security of the law would suffer seriously if expulsions were not subject to reparations. Otherwise the forced displacement of populations would in the future be perceived as a politically acceptable option, and the victims would be left without a recourse.

32. There is a persistent attitude that downplays the expulsion of the Germans and subjects the victims to inacceptable discrimination. In this context Article 26 of the UN Covenant on Civil and Political Rights reminds us that equality before the law is guaranteed for all persons, and any arbitrary discrimination is forbidden. The disregard of the status of the expellees as victims can be understood as a violation of the Covenant's Article 16 which guarantees the right to recognition everywhere as a person before the law. Advocacy of the expulsion or negationism of the attendant crimes can moreover be taken as a violation of Article 20 of the Covenant if motivated by racial hatred or in those cases where incitement to hatred, humiliation or

---

31 Eckart Klein, *Diplomatischer Schutz im Hinblick auf Konfiskation deutschen Vermögens durch Polen*, Bonn 1992. Dieter Blumenwitz, *Das Offenhalten der Vermögensfrage in den deutsch-polnischen Beziehungen*, Bonn 1992.

discrimination is intended. At the very least such downplaying of the crimes also violates Article 17 which forbids the infringement of a person's honor and reputation.[32] The German expellees and their descendants cannot be treated as second class victims and their suffering cannot be simply dismissed. This entails what has been termed the "crime of silence". The continued discrimination against the expellees in the media, school books, museums and in political dialogue entails an assault against basic norms of human rights and human dignity.

33. The legal position of the German Government with respect to the expulsion had gradually weakened since the mid 1990s. Previously each German government has declared that the expulsion of Germans after World War Two, along with their uncompensated confiscation of property, would not be legally recognized. Yet, these Governments failed to take the necessary measures to vindicate the rights of the expellees and to enforce their legitimate claims pursuant to applicable norms of international law and existing mechanisms.

34. Ironically, it was the rigid attitude of the Polish government which has finally stabilized the legal position of the German government concerning the property of the expellees. In 2006 and 2007 Poland's Prime Minister Jaroslav Kaczynski asked German Chancellor Angela Merkel explicitly to recognize the expropriations of the expellees, asserting that the German Federal government must openly declare that all demands for restitution be directed solely to Germany. Chancellor Merkel was not ready to do so.[33] Unlike

---

32 Jakob Th. Möller and Alfred de Zayas: *United Nations Human Rights Committee Case Law: A Handbook. N. P. Engel Publishers, Kehl and Straßburg, 2009.*
33 October 30, 2006, during a state visit to German Chancellor Angela Merkel by Jaroslav Kaczynski in Berlin, where a four hour long exchange took place between the two heads of government. Beside the problem of the Baltic Sea pipeline, the difficulties of German expellee property were a major topic. According to reliable media reports Merkel renewed her position not to support a domestic restitution for expellees. Similarly, demands by Poland for "Germany's renunciation of remedies through international law for expellee restitution" by means of an "international Agreement", were rejected with the words: "Not the right solution." At the end Kaczysnki delared: "In Poland's view this matter is not yet concluded." (Quotations from the German Press Agency ("dpa") and "Focus" magazine.) This exchange of unchanged positions was repeated in similar fashion when Merkel visited Warsaw on March 6, 2007.

its stance toward expellee property, the German government—confirmed in contractual assurances concluded in the early 1990s—has held fast to its goal of recovering German cultural artifacts taken as booty by eastern European states in 1945. Since the mid 1990s, within the realm of international civil law, the protection of property rights with respect to works of art has been significantly strengthened. Even ordinary irregularities in the purchase of artworks by museums more than 70 years ago now lead time and again to uncontested surrender of disputed objects. This is good news for the German expellees and the innumerable artworks they lost in the context of the expulsion and arbitrary confiscations of their private property.

35.

Matters of German public property reveal a special peculiarity in expellee matters. Unlike private property, the German government or other public entities could have effectively renounced their ownership rights to Reich (or other German public) property in Poland, the former East German Provinces and Czechoslovakia. But that has never happened. When the eastern territories treaties were being negotiated, the Social Democratic government avoided the subject in order to maintain their then still earnestly argued position that the recognition of borders had nothing to do with questions of property. The Kohl government saw no occasion to advance the matter and later governments have apparently simply overlooked the question. As a result, it can be established that a valid German legal position in the question of expellee property exists now as before, even if weakened by certain acts and omissions of the German government.

Conclusions

36. All victims have the same human rights. All have a claim to recognition and solidarity, independent of their nationality. Human rights treaties stipulate that all victims shall be treated with respect. The attempt to allow entire groups of victims to fade away, to downplay certain crimes or even conceal them is more than a mere merciless act. It is the expression of an attitude that rejects the universality of human rights, an attitude in which a latent danger lingers. The silence surrounding the expulsion of the Germans transgresses the very ethos of scholarship. 14 to 15 million German expellees and two million dead may today be a cold statistic, yet behind those numbers are the shadows of human faces, the fates of individual people who deserved rights and protection.

37. There are no humane "transfers" of population. The concept entails an oxymoron, a self-contradiction, because the imposed loss of one's homeland can never be humane.[34] Expulsion is mostly racism and always terror. It cannot be excused under any circumstances. Therefore the Czechoslovakian Beneš Decrees, the Yugoslavian AVNOJ decisions, and the Polish Bierut Decrees are irreconcilable with international and European minimal standards of human rights. They should be condemned and formally abrogated.

38. The expulsion of the Germans is among the most portentous events in recent European history for it extinguished a community of co-operation between Slavs and Germans that had grown through many centuries. The economic, moral and cultural consequences of this historical *caesura* have still not been overcome despite the eastward expansion of the

---

[34] "There is no greater sorrow on Earth than the loss of one's native land." Euripides, *Medea*, Chorus, Verses 650–651.

European Union in 2004. Therefore it cannot be simply parenthetical to a common European perception. Nevertheless there still exists a taboo concerning this subject matter which constricts both research and open discussion.

39. It is the scholarly and moral duty of historians to conduct methodically correct research and describe historical events through objective determination of facts and ordering these into a greater context. It is unworthy of a free society and the spirit of free inquiry when contemporary historians, who in serious and exacting method examine subjects of politically disputed themes, are subjected to criticism that would impute to them political or unscholarly motivation, as if they merely served a "reckoning" or "apology" for other crimes. The picture of an epoch would be inevitably falsified if due to political pressures certain fields of study were ignored, or if scholarly discourse were allowed only within a predetermined "politically correct", skewed, intellectually dishonest manner. In its general comment Number 34, the United Nations Human Rights Committee vindicated the right to freedom of research and access to information, including freedom from manipulation or indoctrination, freedom from government imposition of exclusively only one version of historical events. This important general comment on freedom of opinion and expression stipulates in part: "Laws that penalize the expression of opinions about historical facts are incompatible with the obligations that the Covenant imposes on States parties in relation to the respect for freedom of opinion and expression. The Covenant does not permit general prohibition of expressions of an erroneous opinion or an incorrect interpretation of past events."[35] And yet, notwithstanding clearly applicable human rights norms, there is a phenomenon of intimidation, censorship and self-censorship that still hinders open debate on the expulsion of the central and east European Germans.

40. There are many causes of the expulsion and they existed long before the start of World War Two or Hitler's assumption of power on January 30, 1933. Among these are the interests and agendas of the

---

35 CCPR/C/GC/34, adopted on 21 July 2011, para 49.

responsible states and politicians who were active participants in the expulsion[36], the calculated power politics of Stalin, the absurdities and injustices of the Treaties of Versailles, St. Germain and Trianon of 1919 as well as nationalist and pan-Slavic movements dating to the 19th Century. To reduce the causes of the expulsion to the politics of Hitler is historical misrepresentation and manipulation.

41. The expulsion cannot be understood as a punishment of those expelled. The task of punishing those actually guilty of aggression and war crimes was the duty of the Nuremberg Trials and later duty of the general courts. The judgments of the Nuremberg Tribunal established a new principle of international law, namely the personal penal responsibility of politicians and soldiers. The Germans of the eastern territories and the Sudeten Germans were driven from their homes without a thought to their personal guilt. Any punishment that does not take personal responsibility or extenuating circumstances into account is not punishment, but rather vulgar blatant injustice. One should also not forget that many expelled Sudeten Germans were not just totally innocent but had been friends and promoters of Czech-German cooperation and many of them suffered considerably because of their opposition to Hitler.

42. There is no collective guilt. The notion of collective guilt is, as British thinker and publisher Victor Gollancz appropriately noted, "a nonsensical, illiberal, anti-Christian and lamentable Nazi idea."[37] Guilt, like innocence and merit, is always personal and never collective. Therefore the principle of collective guilt cannot be cited in support of the expulsion or the war itself. The decades long debates about the guilt of entire countries for starting the First or Second World Wars are basically wrong in their approach.

---

36 Professor Andreas Hillgruber has formulated it quite accurately when indicating that "the expulsions were not only a reaction to National Socialist provocation but corresponded to long standing conceptions and aspirations, which became achievable in warfare". *Der Zusammenbruch im Osten 1944/45 als Problem der deutschen Nationalgeschichte und der europäischen Geschichte*, a lecture delivered before the Rheinisch-Westfällische Akademie der Wissenschaften on 17 April 1985 in Düsseldorf, published by Westdeutscher Verlag, Opladen, 1985, p. 7.
37 Victor Gollancz, *Stimme aus dem Chaos*, Zurich p. 320

German expellees in devastated Berlin, summer 1945

The question to be examined must always be: who are the responsible individual participants? Up to the present day many Czechs still raise the accusation of collective guilt against "those" Germans, the Sudeten Germans, an attitude no more convincing than the Nazis similar accusations against "the" Jews. The late Czech President Vaclav Havel suggested that there is indeed no collective guilt, but there is also no collective innocence either. His idea found no footing in the debate regarding German collective guilt. Considering the historical facts, the Sudeten German-Czech conflict remains a delicate subject from the Czech point of view. The presumption of innocence is basic to the law of every civilized nation. There does indeed exist a collective morality which binds us all to humane conduct in our relationships.

43. Discussion of the expulsion of the Germans has an eminent importance in today's world. It is not a closed chapter in history, not least demonstrated by the historical mortgage that continues to encumber German-Polish relations. German concessions drawn up to the point of self-renunciation have still not been able to master the unreconstructed relationship between Poland and Germany, one fraught with the trauma of expulsion, expropriation and border changes. Without a readiness to address all issues surrounding the expulsion, without a sincere quest for historical truth, without a just reappraisal of the expulsion, true reconciliation cannot be achieved.

44. The search for a clear path to recognition and enforcement of the right to the homeland along with a just balance to the difficult question of property rights must be intensified in the political sphere. The mere fact that return of Jewish property in Poland is ultimately blocked by the mortgage of the expulsion and expropriation of the Germans, proves how little the expulsion issue can can be grasped through any traditional right vs. left political template. International law is as indivisible as morality itself. A new sense of trust between Poland and Germany, furthering European co-operation, more justice for the victims of the Holocaust as well as for the German expellees, but also legal security for Poland, all are important goals justifying continuing and persevering efforts toward genuine reconciliation. The German expellees must be included in these endeavors.

45. The expulsion and spoliation of the Germans 1944–1948 remains the largest expulsion calamity in history. As such it remains quite contemporary because this unreconstructed precedent has induced and still induces more expulsions in the world, in recent years primarily in the Balkans and in Africa. These must also be condemned by the international community and rectified.[38] A new and more just world order for the 21st Century demands above all historical honesty and objectivity. It is to be hoped that a new unbiased generation of historians and politicians in each of the nations concerned, including the United States, Great Britain, France, Russia, Poland,

---

38 On May 28, 1995 the first UN High Commissioner for Human rights, Dr. José Ayala Lasso, said: "I submit that if in the years following the Second World War the States had reflected more on the implications of the enforced flight and the expulsion of the Germans, today‹s demographic catastrophes, particularly those referred to as 'ethnic cleansing', would, perhaps, not have occurred to the same extent." Dieter Blumenwitz, *50 Jahre Flucht, Deportation, Vertreibung*, Bonn 1995. ISBN 3-925103-77-5. See also Alfred de Zayas, *Nemesis at Potsdam*, Picton Press, 6. ed. 2003, pp. 183–185 and page 40 of this book.

the Czech and Slovak Republics, Hungary, Slovenia, Croatia and Serbia shall recognize the expulsion of the Germans in all its historical implications, and its tragedy. Being good neighbors requires mutual frankness, preparedness to identify mistakes so that truth might have room to grow. In a European Union based on the general validity of human rights, this should be self-evident.

46. The artificial perpetrator/victim template is not just a falsification of history but also a violation of human rights in its flagrant disregard for the dignity of individual persons. It is grotesque to classify millions of German expellees as somehow "guilty" for Hitler's crimes, as "co-perpetrators" of the Holocaust or to ignore their personal suffering because they supposedly belong to a "generation of criminals". These are terms from the dictionary of barbarians, with a totalitarian bent. The expellees were victims of the inhumanity of the victorious powers, and today they are the victims of silence and victims of defamation in many media and among historians trapped in this unnatural Zeitgeist.

47. The sequels of the German expellee tragedy down to our own days must still be researched and discussed, for example the effect of the trauma suffered by millions of raped women and orphaned children. The spiritual and psychological consequences regarding the loss of homeland for the children and grandchildren of the expellees are subjects only lately being addressed by scholars, likewise the grave and enduring consequences of these events among the States and peoples who peripherally benefitted from the expulsion.

48. The phenomenon of expulsion is not an exclusively German problem. Hundreds of thousands of Armenians, Greeks and Assyrian Christians were expelled and massacred during and shortly after the First World War. Greek Cypriots were driven into southern Cyprus in 1974. In the 1990s Kosovars, Bosnians, Croatians and Albanians were expelled by the Serbs, but also many Serbs were driven out of Krajina by Croatians. Today people in Africa (Darfur, Sudan; Democratic Republic of the Congo) are being expelled. A phenomenon closely bound to the injustice of expulsion is being used in an attempt to change the ethnic composition of countries by means of resettlement policies. The Nazis tried this in—among other places—the Polish Warthe (Warta) region, and the Wielkopolska (Greater Poland) territory. An attempt to shift ethnic borders in order to create a homogenous, ethnocentric "national soil", is a pseudo-argument for the shifting of national borders, a chimera, and unsustainable in terms of human rights and international law.

49. The expulsion of the Germans deserves recognition as a scholarly interdisciplinary research objective as it has enormous historical and juridical significance and also lasting demographic, sociological, philosophical and cultural implications and consequences. Within this complex of study and research there are now as before many bright spots. Dissertations and doctoral theses are gradually investigating aspects of it. Countless facets remain to be explored.

50. Prevention is always better than cure. In order to avert any future "ethnic cleansing" anywhere in the world, strategies must be developed, including the normative recognition of the right to one's homeland in the form of an internationally enforceable treaty, the creation of monitoring mechanisms and early warning indicators, as well as a concerted application of the United Nations Declaration on the Illegality of Mass Population Transfers (see below). A fundamental discussion of all aspects of the expulsion of the Germans in its general European and human rights context on grounds just and reasonable to all sides, coupled with meaningful efforts to overcome the unjust consequences, would further such prevention. The Centre Against Expulsions and the Foundation "*Flucht, Vertreibung, Versöhnung*" (flight, expulsion, reconciliation) in Berlin can perform a significant contribution if they are genuinely committed to historical truth and to the enforcement of international law without discrimination.

Professor Alfred de Zayas
Geneva School of Diplomacy
www.afreddezayas.com
zayas@bluewin.ch

Statement of the UN High Commissioner for Human Rights, José Ayala Lasso

Given at the ceremony held at the Paulskirche, Frankfurt, on 28 May 1995 on occasion of the 50th anniversary of the expulsion of about 15 million ethnic Germans from Eastern and Central Europe.

At this historic Church of St. Paul many have already spoken about human rights and democracy. This is good, because our commitment to the *dignitas humana* needs reaffirmation everywhere and on every occasion.

Fifty years after the end of the Second World War, we see that new wars and grave human rights violations continue to take their toll in lives, cause major refugee movements, deprive men and women of their rights and render them homeless.

Also fifty years ago the United Nations Organization was founded with the noble aims of maintaining international peace and security and promoting and protecting human rights throughout the world. The Organization has worked hard, achieved many successes, but also experienced serious disappointments. The United Nations and I myself as High Commissioner for Human Rights will devote all of our energies to make these goals reality.

Over the past fifty years the General Assembly has adopted *inter alia* the Universal Declaration of Human Rights, the Covenant on Civil and Political Rights, the Covenant on Economic, Social and Cultural Rights, the Convention on the Elimination of all Forms of Racial Discrimination, and the Convention against Torture. In this perspective, it is clear that ethnic cleansing, expulsion and involuntary transfers of population violate many of the fundamental human rights enshrined in these Conventions.

The right not to be expelled from one's homeland is a fundamental right. The Sub-Commission on Prevention of Discrimination and Protection of Minorities is currently seised of the question of the human rights dimensions of population transfers. The newest report of Special Rapporteur Awn Shawkat Al-Khasawneh concludes that population transfers violate the human rights of both transferred and receiving populations (E/CN.4/Sub.2/1994/18).

The United Nations International Law Commission is also currently examining this important question. In Article 21 of the Draft Code of Crimes against the Peace and Security of Mankind the expulsion of persons from their homeland is referred to as a gross and systematic violation of human rights and as an international crime. In Article 22 of the Code population expulsions and collective punishments against the civilian population are listed among the gravest war crimes.

The most recent statement of the United Nations on the Right to the homeland was given on 26 August 1994 by the Sub-Commission, which in its Resolution 1994/24 affirmed the right of persons to remain in peace in their own homes, on their own lands and in their own countries. Moreover, the Resolution affirms the right of refugees and displaced persons to return in safety and dignity, to their country of origin.

I submit that if in the years following the Second World War the States had reflected more on the implications of the enforced flight and the expulsion of the Germans, today's demographic catastrophes, particularly those referred to as "ethnic cleansing", would, perhaps, not have occurred to the same extent.

In this context I should like to refer to the Charter of the German Expellees. It is good that men and women who have suffered injustice are prepared to break the vicious circle of revenge and reprisals and devote themselves in peaceful ways to seek the recognition of the right to the homeland and work toward reconstruction and integration in Europe. One day this peaceful approach will receive the recognition it deserves.

There is no doubt that during the Nazi occupation the peoples of Central and Eastern Europe suffered enormous injustices that cannot be forgotten. Accordingly they had a legitimate claim for reparation. However, legitimate claims ought not to be enforced through collective punishment on the basis of general discrimination and without a determination of personal guilt. In the Nuremberg and Tokyo trials the crucial principle of personal responsibility for crimes was wisely applied. It is worthwhile to reread the Nuremberg protocols and judgment.

Our goal remains the universal recognition of human rights, which are based on the principle of the equality of all human beings. Indeed, all victims of war and injustice deserve our respect and compassion, since every individual human life is precious. It is our duty to continue our endeavors in the name of the *dignitas humana.*

José Ayala Lasso, first United Nations High Commissioner for Human Rights (1994–1997)

Speech to the German expellees, Day of the Homeland, Berlin 6 August 2005.

Ten years ago, on the occasion of the fiftieth anniversary of the end of the Second World War and the beginning of the expulsion of 15 million Germans from their homelands in the East, you invited me to participate in the commemoration that was held on May 28th, 1995 at the Paulskirche in Frankfurt am Main.

Although I was unable to come personally, since my functions as High Commissioner for Human Rights required me at that particular time to be in Rwanda, I did send a statement to you, which I understand was read out in German translation and subsequently published by the late Professor Dieter Blumenwitz.

In that statement I recalled the resolutions of the United Nations Sub-Commission on Promotion and Protection of Human Rights, in particular

José Ayala Lasso speaking
in Berlin, August 6, 2005

concerning the right to live in one's homeland and the right to return in safety and dignity to one's homeland.

We all remember that in 1995 the war in the former Yugoslavia had already produced hundreds of thousands of refugees and that a policy known as «ethnic cleansing» had been put into effect, a new term to refer to an old and very cruel State practice, that of terrorizing a civilian population and forcing men, women and children to abandon their homes and flee to the unknown.

Although the war in Yugoslavia has ended, the world does not appear to be any safer, and human beings continue to be subjected to the ravages of unjust wars and unjust peace settlements.

One of my successors as High Commissioner for Human Rights, Sergio Vieira de Mello, gave his life in the struggle for a better world when, in his capacity as representative of the Secretary General in Baghdad, he perished in August 2003, in the gravest attack ever endured by the United Nations. I bow my head before his memory.

I am convinced that the United Nations and, in particular, the Office of the High Commissioner for Human Rights, currently under the able leadership of Judge Louise Arbour, will persevere in its patient task of building a universal culture of human rights. Over the past sixty years the United Nations has performed a monumental job of codification of norms. Expert organs have been established to monitor compliance with those norms. Procedures have been developed to allow individuals to invoke their rights before those organs. Civil society and non-governmental organizations have actively contributed and continue to participate in this process. All this legal achievements are important, but the success of the human rights system very much depends on the commitment of civil society and the development of national human rights institutions and infrastructures.

We are now engaged in a transcendental exercise to reform and modernize the UN System. One of the basic pillars of that reform is to strengthen the Commission of Human Rights. As the UN Secretary General has recently said, the Universal Declaration of Human Rights continues to be one of the most important achievements of the world organization. A new vision of collective security is emerging everywhere and everybody recognizes the links between poverty and insecurity, respect for human rights and peace. That is why in his report to the UN Secretary General, the group of experts created by Mr. Kofi

Annan to make proposals to respond to the challenges of the New Millennium, suggested to reform the Human Rights Commission and to create a Council of Human Rights with universal composition and full responsibilities for the promotion and protection of all human rights.

I think that the grave problems related to democracy, development, governability, collective security, fight against terrorism, international relations, are pointing to the need to better promote and protect human rights. If we really want to create a new international order, we must recognize that it is urgent and imperative to look forward to a new conscience regarding the supremacy of human rights. A new humanism must emerge and we must all, individually and collectively, contribute to the foundations of this new era.

The realization of human rights remains a great challenge to all of us, since the enforcement of the norms depends on the political will of the States. There is, of course, no nobler task than to work for the realization of all human rights.

Among the collective rights, the right to self-determination is, of course, of particular relevance to all of us. The United Nations played an important role in the process of decolonization in Asia and Africa, and in the abolition of Apartheid. Other collective rights, including the rights of minorities, and the right to one's homeland have not been fully realized. Of course, the right to one's homeland is not merely a collective right, but it is also an individual right and a precondition for the exercise of many civil, political, economic, social and cultural rights.

It was during my tenure as High Commissioner for Human Rights that the Sub-Commission on Promotion and Protection of Human Rights carried out an important study on "The Human Rights Dimensions of Population Transfers", and that an expert conference met in Geneva, chaired by the Sub-Commission's Rapporteur, Awn Shawkat Al Khasawneh, today Judge at the International Court of Justice. In his final Report to the Sub-Commission (E/CN.4/Sub.2/1997/23) Judge Al Khasawneh concluded that the right to one's homeland was a fundamental human right and that States are not entitled to displace populations forcibly from their native soil. In the Declaration appended to his report, we read "Every person has the right to remain in peace, security and dignity in one's home, or on one's land and in one's country" (Art. 4, para. 1). We also read "Every person has the right to return voluntarily, and in safety and dignity, to the country of origin and, within it, to the place of origin or choice." (Art. 8)

Even if we are still far from achieving these goals, even if there are millions of homeless persons in the world today, it is important to reaffirm these basic principles and to seek ways and means to implement them. This is why I also endorse the idea of establishing an international Centre against population transfers which would not only document and study past expulsions, but would also endeavor to prevent future expulsions anywhere in the world by educating and raising consciousness about the horrors of forced population transfers, by developing early-warning strategies, and by contributing to United Nations activities in this field. I am persuaded that Berlin would be an appropriate place for such a Centre.

I believe that the example of the German expellees is particularly telling. While we acknowledge the magnitude of the expulsion and the sorrow over the loss of provinces that had been the homeland of Immanuel Kant, Arthur Schopenhauer, Johann Gottfried Herder, Joseph von Eichendorff, and others, we must also recognize the considerable sacrifice made by the expellees in choosing the path of peaceful integration. We cannot but admire the moral fiber of these people, the wisdom of their leaders, who renounced any and all forms of violence, who decided to build a new homeland in the West, without, however, abandoning their love for their origins, for the landscapes where they grew up, the churches and temples where they worshiped, the cemeteries where their ancestors are buried.

I take this occasion today to recall the «Charter of the Expellees» promulgated in Stuttgart on 5 August 1950. In this important Charter, the victims of expulsion formally renounced «all thought of revenge and retaliation. Our resolution is a solemn and sacred one, in memory of the infinite suffering brought upon mankind, particularly during the past decade.» This renunciation effectively broke the vicious circle of reprisal and counter-reprisal. The Charter also committed the expellees to work for the reconstruction of Germany and of Europe, which one day should be united. A remarkable document indeed.

The Office of the High Commissioner for Refugees frequently quotes a line from the chorus of Euripides' *Medea* (verse 650–651): "There is no greater sorrow on Earth than the loss of one's native land."

As former High Commissioner for Human Rights, I would add that we have an obligation to assuage this sorrow, to show compassion to the victims of expulsion, to assist them in preserving their culture and identity, to provide a measure of relief and, if possible, facilitate their peaceful repatriation. As I said in 1995, the right to one's homeland is a fundamental human right that the entire world community is called upon to respect. If persons have been forced to leave their homelands, they should be given the option and the opportunity to return.

Admittedly, there can be conflicting claims to the same homeland. With good will and international assistance, such conflicts can be solved peacefully, allowing the enjoyment of the right to the homeland by all who love their roots. Indeed, love of homeland is a positive value. Only those who love their homeland will work to improve it, to make it a better place for their children and grandchildren and to integrate it in a higher concept of world solidarity.

Sixty years ago the victorious Powers assembled in Berlin to plan the post-war world. At the Potsdam Conference they discussed the challenge of peace-making, and they also were confronted with the huge logistical and humanitarian problems arising from millions of internally displaced persons, Germans from East Prussia, Pomerania, Silesia, who had fled before the onslaught of the Soviet Army and other millions who had remained in their homeland and were being expelled in that cruel summer of 1945. We bow our heads before the victims of Nazi aggression in the East. At the same time, we cannot remain insensitive to the suffering of innocent men, women and children from East Prussia, Pomerania, Silesia, Sudetenland and other areas, who became victims of the unjust and immoral principle of collective punishment.

The Nuremberg Trials were convened in 1945 to vindicate the principle of individual criminal responsibility, and to punish those political leaders who unleashed aggressive war and who ordered the commission of war crimes and crimes against humanity. Among the crimes for which the National Socialist leaders were indicted and convicted were the crime of forced population transfer and the crime of deportation to forced labor. The Nuremberg judgment was approved by the General Assembly in 1946, and subsequently the International Law Commission was entrusted with the task of formulating a code on crimes against peace and security of mankind. In articles 18 and 20 of the draft code adopted in 1996, mass expulsion and deportation to forced labor are defined as war crimes and crimes against humanity. More recently, the Diplomatic Conference of Rome adopted the 1998 statute of the International Criminal Court, which in articles 7 and 8 similarly condemns the crime of expulsion. The creation of the International Criminal Court is a considerable step toward the strengthening of the rule of law in the sphere of international relations. Any attempt to weaken the Rome Statute or to ignore its significance must be strongly opposed and criticized.

Meanwhile the International Criminal Tribunal for the Former Yugoslavia has been prosecuting those responsible for the implementation of the policy of ethnic cleansing. In a very real sense the trial against Slobodan Milosevic is a trial to vindicate the right to the homeland, and not only the right to the homeland of the Bosnians, of the Croats and of the Kosovars, but ultimately also of the Serbs of the Krajina. Important international case-law will no doubt emerge from the trials currently being conducted in The Hague.

Let me conclude with a reflection on the notion of human rights, a notion as old as humanity, even though only very gradually articulated, in the Bible, in the writings of the Chinese, Indian and Greek philosophers, in the works of Jean Jacques Rousseau, in the French and American declarations of the eighteenth century, long before the advent of the League of Nations with its system of protection of minority rights and of the United Nations with its Commission of Human Rights.

This notion so dear to us rests on a broader respect for all living beings, and on the belief in the equality in dignity and rights of all humans, regardless of their color, origin, religion and social status. From this basis, modern societies develop the concepts of solidarity and interdependence. We cannot be indifferent to violations of human rights, wherever they happen. That is why we must fight against poverty and injustice, everywhere.

As a Latin American I strongly support the exercise of all human rights by the indigenous populations. One important step in the long development of human rights concepts was the long-lasting dispute in the Council of the Indies in Spain, in the Sixteenth Century, whether the indigenous of America were human beings. Two Dominicans, Bartolomé de las Casas and Fray Antonio de Montesinos argued before the Habsburg Emperor Charles V that the indigenous populations were human beings who had souls and rights. As a result of their interventions, laws were enacted to protect the rights of the indigenous, which were essentially human rights laws. And even if these laws were violated with impunity, an awareness of right and wrong was awakened.

We should remember that the indigenous peoples of America, they too, had a right to their homeland, and that they were deprived of their lands and property by force and reduced to the condition of near slavery.

We are facing in Latin America a new form of an ancient problem. In the past, the world community has taken measures against the enforced transfer of populations. Now we are experiencing the transfer of populations by the

Angela Merkel—a few weeks before becoming German Chancellor—giving thanks to José Ayala Lasso after his speech. Sitting in the center: Erika Steinbach, President of the German Federation of Expellees ("Bund der Vertriebenen").

way of massive emigration, due to the deterioration of economic and social conditions in many countries, including my country Ecuador. More than 20% of the total population has emigrated in the past three or four years. The consequences for the homeland are dramatic and, no doubt, the situation affects also the countries of destination of these massive migrations. I encourage the Commission of Human Rights to study this problem from the new optic of solidarity in the protection of human rights.

The promotion and protection of human rights is a permanent fight to recognize and respect human dignity. We cannot be indifferent to this noble cause. In the past, much progress has been achieved thanks to the combined work of the United Nations, international organizations, non-governmental organizations and civil society. But the work must be permanent and demands the participation of all human beings.

Thus I encourage you to persevere in your commitment to human rights, and to continue working so that all human rights and, certainly, the right to one's homeland, be universally recognized and respected. In this way we will be contributing to the establishment of a new world order based on basic principles of dignity and justice for all.

I would like to thank your organization and each one of you for giving all your devotion and activity to this fight for human dignity. I think that you are giving a good example to the world and what you are doing is going to be good not simply for Germany or Europe but for the whole world, because it is, of course, the spirit which conducts human beings to good ways, and it is the activity of the spirit which will bring us to a new world: just, free, democratic, developed and progressive.

I thank you for your kind attention.

Declaration on Population Transfer and the Implantation of Settlers

Article 1

This Declaration sets standards which are applicable in all situations, including peacetime, disturbances and tensions, internal violence, internal armed conflict, mixed internal-international armed conflict, international armed conflict and public emergency situations. The norms contained in this Declaration must be respected under all circumstances.

Article 2

These norms shall be respected by, and are applicable to all persons, groups and authorities, irrespective of their legal status.

Article 3

Unlawful population transfers entail a practice or policy having the purpose or effect of moving persons into or out of an area, either within or across an international border, or within, into or out of an occupied territory, without the free and informed consent of the transferred population and any receiving population.

Article 4

1. Every person has the right to remain in peace, security and dignity in one's home, or on one's land and in one's country.
2. No person shall be compelled to leave his place of residence.
3. The displacement of the population or parts thereof shall not be ordered, induced or carried out unless their safety or imperative military reasons so demand. All persons thus displaced shall be allowed to return to their homes, lands, or places of origin immediately upon cessation of the conditions which made their displacement imperative.

Article 5

The settlement, by transfer or inducement, by the Occupying Power of parts of its own civilian population into the territory it occupies or by the Power exercising de facto control over a disputed territory is unlawful.

Article 6

Practices and polices having the purpose or effect of changing the demographic composition of the region in which a national, ethnic, linguistic, or other minority or an indigenous population is residing, whether by deportation, displacement, and/or the implantation of settlers, or a combination thereof, are unlawful.

Article 7

Population transfers or exchanges of population cannot be legalized by international agreement when they violate fundamental human rights norms or peremptory norms of international law.

Article 8

Every person has the right to return voluntarily, and in safety and dignity, to the country of origin and, within it, to the place of origin or choice. The exercise of the right to return does not preclude the victim's right to adequate remedies, including restoration of properties of which they were deprived in connection with or as a result of population transfers, compensation for any property that cannot be restored to them, and any other reparations provided for in international law.

Article 9

The above practices of population transfer constitute internationally wrongful acts giving rise to State responsibility and to individual criminal liability.

Article 10

Where acts or omissions prohibited in the present Declaration are committed, the international community as a whole and individual States, are under an obligation: (a) not to recognize as legal the situation created by such acts;

(b) in ongoing situations, to ensure the immediate cessation of the act and the reversal of the harmful consequences; (c) not to render aid, assistance or support, financial or otherwise, to the State which has committed or is committing such act in the maintaining or strengthening of the situation created by such act.

Article 11

States shall adopt measures aimed at preventing the occurrence of population transfers and the implantation of settlers, including the prohibition of incitement to racial, religious or linguistic hatred.

Article 12

Nothing in these articles shall be construed as affecting the legal status of any authorities, groups or persons involved in situations of internal violence, disturbances, tensions or public emergency.

Article 13

1. Nothing in these articles shall be construed to restrict or impair the provisions of any international humanitarian or human rights instruments.
2. In case of different norms applicable to the same situation, the standard offering maximum protection to persons and groups subjected to population transfers shall prevail.

UN Doc. E/CN.4/Sub.2/1997/23.

Greeting to the German Expellees from Pope John Paul II

His Holiness

Pope John Paul II

sends his heartfelt blessings

to the participants at the "Day of the Homeland" in Berlin

With great interest the Holy Father has learned that the League of German Expellees, on September 6, 2003 in Berlin, is celebrating its "Day of the Homeland" under the motto "Europe Unites through Human Rights".

In its recent past Europe has had to endure inhuman ideologies and terrible conflict among nations, all exacerbated by overwrought nationalisms that fueled the awful tragedies of two world wars. The Day of the Homeland is dedicated to the memory of all those who were violently torn from their hereditary roots by the destructive powers of hatred and vengeance; "they wandered, finding no way to a city where they could settle" (Psalm 107:4). No one knows better than those affected how painful it is to be deprived of, how precious the basic right is to live in the land of one's childhood, to reassure one's sense of heritage at the gravesites of ancestors, to be rooted among one's countrymen and thus enabling fulfillment in the joy of life and self confidence. Respect for this very human right contributes authoritatively to the formation of a just and humane world.

And yet, striving after happiness and fulfillment goes far beyond that which man can achieve of his own volition. It is a gift of God to be redeemed in eternity: "Our home is in heaven" (Philippians 3:20). This certainty gives Christians and all men of good will the inner freedom, the ultimate tools to be used responsibly for a genuine construction of peace and justice, all the while mindful that as a "guest on earth" one treads a path to the house of the eternal Father.

With the certain belief in a Europe of united and reconciled nations, His Holiness Pope John Paul II gives his apostolic blessings to the organizers and delegates at this year's Day of the Homeland convened by the League of German Expellees.

Greeting to the German Expellees from Pope Benedict XVI

To the participants at the Day of the Homeland in Berlin, 2005

His holiness Pope Benedict XVI has learned that the League of German Expellees is celebrating a Day of the Homeland in Berlin on August 6. The Holy Father sends its participants his blessings and assures them of his spiritual support.

To this day the experience of violent expulsion remains a horrible reality for untold numbers of people. The summons to "outlaw expulsion worldwide" is directed to all mankind, for it is the salutary rootedness in homeland that enables people joy in their lives, social order and hope for the future.

The concept of homeland has geographical, cultural, spiritual and religious dimensions. It belongs to any people and their history and cannot be therefore violently seized. Ideologies that promote expulsion or in any way seek to justify it violate the dignity of man.

In the belief that people and nations are nourished by the spirit and power of the Gospel of Jesus Christ and its will to peace, His Holiness Pope Benedict XVI prays that all participants at this year's Day of the Homeland receive from the heart of God His everlasting protection and rich blessing.

Losses due to the expulsion of the Germans 1944–1948

The Allied authorities that administered the Zones of occupied Germany 1945–49 as well as the statistical authorities of the Federal Republic of Germany and the German Democratic Republic attempted to estimate the number of Germans who had been evacuated, who had fled or who had been subsequently expelled from the former German provinces as well as from Poland, Czechoslovakia, Hungary and Yugoslavia. It was a particularly difficult task to estimate the number of deaths, since there was a high number of "missing" or "disappeared" persons whose fate could not been determined.

After years of demographic studies, the German federal statistical office *(Statistisches Bundesamt)* in Wiesbaden in 1958 issued a final report, estimating a demographic loss of some 2.225 million German civilians in all of Central and Eastern Europe. The figures listed in the table below are from this report[39]. According to this investigation, the number of 1,099,500 war losses includes 11,500 civilians killed by Allied Strategic Bombing (up until January 31, 1945). Losses due to forced labour among German prisoners of war were registered as "war losses" even if they had occurred after May 8, 1945.

In the Federal Republic of Germany studies on expulsion casualties were also carried out by the German Red Cross, the *Diakonisches Werk*, the *Heimatortskarteien* (which until today operate as registration offices in exile of the old communities affected by the expulsion), the *Gesamterhebung zur Klärung des Schicksals der deutschen Bevölkerung in den Vertreibungsgebieten [Comprehensive Survey for Clearing up the Destiny of the German Population in the Areas of Expulsion]*, and by the historians at the German Federal Archives in Koblenz.

---

[39] *Die deutschen Vertreibungsverluste* [The German Expulsion Casualties]. *Bevölkerungsbilanzen für die deutschen Vertreibungsgebiete 1939/50.* Herausgeber: Statistisches Bundesamt, Wiesbaden. Stuttgart: Verlag W. Kohlhammer, 1958.

At first glance some statistical studies released after the 1958 *Vertreibungsverluste* tables seem to indicate a lower number of casualties resulting from the expulsion. For example the 1965 *Gesamterhebung* gave name-by-name evidence of "only" 473,013 German civilians killed. However, the criterion of this count was extremely restrictive: The person killed had to be seen dead and identified by an eye-witness. Obviously, the witness himself must have survived the expulsion or must have left written evidence in order to be able to report his knowledge to West German investigators of this survey carried out in 1959–1964. However, very many atrocities happened without surviving witnesses, and even the knowledge of eye-witnesses who survived "behind the iron curtain" – in the German Democratic Republic or in Eastern

Description	German Population in 1939	War Deaths	Population growth 1939–50	Remain East Eur USSR
Germany 1937 Borders (Eastern Provinces)	9,575,200	667,500	546,000	1,1
Poland 1939 Borders	1,371,000	108,000	46,000	4
Free City of Danzig	380,000	22,000	22,000	
Czechoslovakia	3,477,000	180,000	235,000	2
Baltic States	249,500	15,000	5,700	
Yugoslavia	536,800	40,000	23,500	
Hungary	623,000	32,000	17,000	3
Romania	786,000	35,000	41,000	4
Total	**16,998,500**	**1,099,500**	**936,200**	**2,71**

Europe – normally could not be integrated in the examination. Furthermore, it should be noted that the 1965 survey also gives name-by-name evidence of another 1,905,991 "unresolved cases". Although this huge number includes missing soldiers, it gives an idea of how far the number of 473,013 falls behind the accurate number of lives lost due to the expulsion.

Another official German examination, carried out in the late 1960s and early 70s by a team of researchers at the German Federal Archives (Bundesarchiv) under the directorship of Dr. Johannes Hopf (whom the author interviewed on several occasions when studying the tens of thousands of testimonies of survivors contained in the Ost-Dokumentation files) and released in 1974, gives a number of 600,000 Germans directly killed during the expulsion. Here as well, only documented crimes were counted, but compared to the 1965 study the rigid criterion of an eye-witness who had seen and identified the dead was removed. So there is no contradiction between the 1965 and 1974 inquiries. However, the 1974 study as well neither registered victims of unreported crimes nor included the huge number of those who perished during or soon after being expelled due to starvation and extreme lack of housing and medical care. These huge losses, clearly caused by the expulsion, can only be "grasped" by a population balance as the one carried out in 1958 by the Statistisches Bundesamt.

Thus, there is no "dark number" of casualties, but a question of interpretation of missing and disappeared persons. The best way of approaching this tragedy is by considering the magnitude of the expulsion and the near impossibility that up to 15 million persons could be "transferred" at the end of a devastating war without causing a humanitarian crisis of prodigious proportions. No one can deny that tens of thousands of ethnic German civilians perished from

lled by 950	Unresolved Cases (post war losses)
,981,000	1,338,700
688,000	185,000
290,800	83,200
,000,400	272,900
169,500	51,400
297,500	135,800
213,000	57,000
253,000	101,000
,893,200	2,225,000

exhaustion, exposure, disease and famine shortly after arrival in the West (as we know from contemporary reports by Robert Murphy, Lucius Clay and other Allied authorities), that countless perished in internment camps awaiting expulsion, and thousands upon thousands during the many years of forced labour in the Soviet Union (these Eastern Germans had been deported East, not West, and many of them were never "expelled", because they died before being released). The figures of the Statistical Bundesamt are largely confirmed by the research of subsequent historians including Gerhard Reichling, who in 1986 and 1989 published a two-volume survey entitled *Die deutschen Vertriebenen in Zahlen*, and by the studies of Dr. Fritz Peter Habel. Lower casualty figures recently suggested by some historians can be attributed to an unwillingness to take into account the large number of deaths that occurred in the war-ravaged German lands west of the Rivers Oder and Neisse which had to absorb the expellees as sequels of the flight and expulsion and the undetermined number of deaths during internment and forced labour.

In 2006 the German government reaffirmed its belief that about 2 million civilians perished in the flight and expulsion from Eastern Europe. On 29 November 2006 State Secretary in the German Federal Ministry of the Interior, Christoph Bergner, outlined the stance of the respective governmental institutions in Deutschlandfunk saying that the numbers presented by the German government and others are not contradictory to the 600,000 estimate [of the 1974 study] as this figure comprises the deaths directly caused by atrocities during the expulsion measures and thus only includes people who on the spot were raped, beaten, or else brought to death, while the two millions estimate also includes people who on their way to post-war Germany perished as a result of epidemics, hunger, cold, air raids and the like, and those who died shortly after arrival at destination.

But leaving statistics aside, each human being who lost his or her life as a result of flight and expulsion had a right to live. And whether 600,000, one million, two millions or even more ethnic Germans perished, they died unjustly and the issues of international law and human rights are the same regardless of the figures. As the report of the UN Sub-Commission on the Promotion and Protection of Human Rights clearly states, forced population transfers constitute a gross violation of human rights.

The Nemmersdorf massacre of October 21, 1944. Countless other massacres would follow.

Charter of the German Expellees

Conscious of their responsibility before God and men, conscious of their affiliation to the Western Christian community, conscious of their German origin, and realizing the common task of all nations of Europe, the elected representatives of millions of expellees, after careful deliberation and after having searched their conscience, have resolved to make public a solemn declaration to the German people and to the entire world, defining both the duties and the rights which the German expellees consider their basic law and an indispensable precondition for the establishment of a free and united Europe.

1. We, the expellees, renounce all thought of revenge and retaliation. Our resolution is solemn and sacred in memory of the infinite suffering brought upon mankind, particularly during the past decade.
2. We shall support with all our strength every endeavor directed towards the establishment of a united Europe in which the nations may live in freedom from fear and coercion.
3. We shall contribute, by hard and untiring work, to the reconstruction of Germany and Europe.

We have lost our homeland. The homeless are strangers on the face of the earth. God himself placed men in their native land. To separate man forcibly from his native land means to kill him in his mind.

We have suffered and experienced this fate. We therefore feel called upon to demand that the right to our native land be recognized and realized as one of the basic rights of man, granted to him by God.

However, as long as this right has not been materialized for us, we do not want to stand aside under imposed inactivity, but rather want to strive and work with all members of our nation in new, purified forms of brotherly and considerate cooperation.

For this reason we claim and demand, today as in the past:

1. Equal rights as citizens, not merely before the law but also in everyday life;
2. Just and reasonable distribution of the burdens of the last war among the entire German people and an honest application of this principle;
3. Reasonable integration of all professional groups of expellees into the life of the German people;
4. Incorporation of the German expellees into the reconstruction work for Europe.

The nations of the world should become sensitive of their co-responsibility for the fate of the expellees who suffer most from the hardships of our times. The nations should act in accordance with their duties and their conscience as Christians.

The nations must realize that the fate of the German expellees, just as that of all refugees, is a world problem the solution of which calls for the highest moral responsibility and for a commitment to tremendous effort.

We therefore call upon all nations and men of good will to join in the mutual endeavor to find a way out of guilt, misfortune, suffering, poverty and misery which will lead us all to a better future.

Stuttgart, August 5, 1950

Proclamation of the Charter, Stuttgart, August 5, 1950.

Telegram of Geoffrey Harrison to John Troutbeck (1st August 1945)

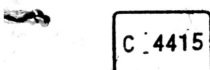

C - 4415

2 AUG 1945

British Delegation,
BERLIN.

1st August, 1945.

My dear Jack,

Transfers of German Populations

You will have seen from the records of the
Conference that a Sub–Committee was set up on July 25th
consisting of Sobolev, Cannon and myself "to consider
and report to the Foreign Secretaries' meeting what
practical arrangements could be made for regulating
transfer of populations in Europe, consequent on the
defeat of Germany".

The Sub–Committee met three times, taking as a
basis of discussion a draft which I circulated.

I attach a copy of the document as it finally
emerged. The negotiations were not easy – no
negotiations with the Russians ever are – but I hope
the result will not be too unsatisfactory. William
Strang and General Weeks are content.

We had a great struggle, which had to be taken
up to the Plenary Meeting, about including the last
three and a half lines. Sobolev took the view that
the Polish and Czechoslovak wish to expel their German
populations was the fulfilment of an historic mission
which the Soviet Government were unwilling to try to
impede. The view of the Soviet Government was that it
was the function of the Allied Control Council in
Germany to facilitate the reception of the transferred
populations as rapidly as possible. Cannon and I
naturally strongly opposed this view. We made it clear
that we did not like the idea of mass transfers anyway.

As/

J.M. Troutbeck, Esq., C.M.G.,
    Foreign Office.

As, however, we could not prevent them, we wished to
ensure that they were carried out in as orderly and
humane a manner as possible and in a way which would
not throw an intolerable burden on the occupying
authorities in Germany. Uncle Joe finally agreed to
join in requesting the Polish and Czech Governments
and the Control Council for Hungary to suspend
expulsions until the report of the Allied Control
Council in Germany was available. This may prevent
mass expulsions for the timebeing, but I have no doubt
that hundreds of Germans will continue to move
westwards daily. Fortunately, the Russians and the
Americans will bear the first brunt of the influx.

We did our best to get some reference to the
absorptive capacity of Germany, but here the Russians
dug their toes in, on the grounds that they at all
events have no doubt whatsoever about Germany's
capacity to absorb millions of transferees. The
position is to some extent safeguarded by the phrase
in paragraph 2 "having regard to the present situation
in Germany".

I think one thing was established at this Conference,
namely that the problem is now not going to be anything
like on the scale we had originally foreseen. The
Poles claim that there are only one to one and a half
million Germans of whom they wish to dispose left
in the area they are taking over up to the Oder-Neisse
line. Benes has two and a half millions and there are
a quarter of a million Schwaben. This makes a grand
total of under four millions. Goodness knows this will
be a big enough problem, and of course the millions of
Germans who lived east of the Oder must have got somewhere.
But people who have been in Germany have got the
impression, rightly or wrongly, that there are fewer
Germans in the Reich than had been supposed. Everyone
agrees that one of the very first things to be done,
as soon as possible, is to take a census, however
rough and ready it may be.

                                                                        You/

You will have seen from telegrams which I sent
off this morning to Paris, Prague and Warsaw that
H.M. Representatives in those countries are being
instructed to concert in communicating to the French,
Polish and Czechoslovak Governments the text of the
Agreement.   The French are being invited to send
appropriate instructions, after the conclusion of
the Conference, to the Commander-in-Chief of the French
forces of occupation in Germany.

It will in addition be necessary for us to
communicate the text of the Agreement officially
to Field-Marshal Montgomery and request him to
concert with his colleagues on the Control Council
in implementing it.   I presume the War Office should
do this as soon as possible.   Will you bring this
to their attention?

The War Office should also be moved to inform
our Representative on the Allied Control Commission
in Hungary of the Berlin Agreement unless this could
be done through Joe Gascoigne (your letter C 4026/95/18
of July 22nd.).

Yours ever

Geoffrey Harrison

Pictures

On May 31, 1945 more than 27,000 Germans were expelled from their centuries-old hometown Brünn (Brno), capital of Moravia. About 5,200 of them died on the 34 miles (55 km) long "Brünn death march". The picture above is an almost unique document of the ethnic cleansing of this city.

Like cattle these Germans were loaded on trucks in the town Böhmisch Aicha (Česky Dub) in Northern Bohemia. The picture is most likely from June or July 1945, as these early expulsions were often carried out by Czech "National Committees". The office of the local committee ("Narodny Vybor") can be seen in the background.

During the year 1946 alone, two million Sudeten Germans were "transferred" from Czechoslovakia. The usual method was to intern the Germans in camps like the one above in the Prague suburb Modrany and deport them following internment of indeterminate duration. People on the picture above are on the way to trains, wearing transportation tags on their necks (1946).

Expellees from Konstantinsbad (a village in Western Bohemia known for its spa) leaving a cargo train in Zellhausen near Offenbach. The people on this 1946 picture survived the expulsion. However, many expellees would die during the months to come due to malnutrition, cold, disease and despair.

Selected Bibliography

Adler, H.G.: Theresienstadt 1941–1945: Das Antlitz einer Zwangsgemeinschaft, Tübingen, 1955.

Andrysek, Oldrich: Report on the Definition of Minorities. The Netherlands Institute of Human Rights, SIM Special No. 8, Utrecht, 1989.

Aurich, Peter: Der deutsch-polnische September 1939, Munich, 1970.

Bacque, James: Crimes and Mercies, Little Brown and Company, London, 1997.

Badenheuer, Konrad: Die Sudetendeutschen – Eine Volksgruppe in Europa, Sudetendeutscher Rat, Munich, 2007. 3rd edition Munich, 2010.

Beneš, Eduard. Memoirs. London, 1954.

Blumenwitz, Dieter: Der Prager Vertrag, Bonn, 1985.

— (ed.): Flucht und Vertreibung, Carl Heymanns Verlag, Cologne, Berlin, 1987.

— Das Offenhalten der Vermögensfrage in den deutsch-polnischen Beziehungen, Bonn, 1992.

— Rechtsgutachten über die Verbrechen an den Deutschen in Jugoslawien, Juristische Studien, Munich, 2002.

Böhme, Kurt: Gesucht Wird. German Red Cross, Munich, 1965.

Borodziej, Wlodzimierz / Hans Lemberg (eds.): „Unsere Heimat ist uns ein fremdes Land geworden…“ Die Deutschen östlich von Oder und Neiße 1945–1950. Dokumente aus polnischen Archiven, Vol. 1–4, Marburg/Lahn, 2000/04.

Bramwell, Anna (ed.): Refugees in the Era of Total War, London, 1988.

Broszat, Martin: Zweihundert Jahre deutsche Polenpolitik, Munich, 1963.

Bruegel, J. W.: Czechoslovakia Before Munich. Cambridge, 1970.

Bundesministerium für Vertriebene, Flüchtlinge und Kriegsgeschädigte (ed.): Dokumentation der Vertreibung der Deutschen aus Ost-Mitteleuropa, Vol. I/1-V, compiled and edited by Theodor Schieder, Hans Rothfels, Bonn (1953–60), dtv reprint, Munich 2004.

Burckhardt, Carl Jacob: Meine Danziger Mission 1937–1939, Munich, 1960, 3rd expanded edition 1980.

Byrnes, James: Speaking Frankly, New York, 1947.

Capotorti, Francesco: Study on the Rights of Persons Belonging to Ethnic, Religious and Linguistic Minorities, UN Doc. E/CN.4/Sub.2/384/Rev.1, 1979.

Churchill, Winston. Closing the Ring, Boston 1951; Triumph and Tragedy, Boston, 1953.

Clay, Lucius: Decision in Germany, New York, 1950.

Conquest, Robert: The Soviet Deportation of Nationalities, London, 1960.

Danube Swabian Association of the USA, Genocide of the Ethnic Germans in Yugoslavia 1944–1948, Chicago, 2000.

Ermacora, Felix: Die sudetendeutschen Fragen, Langen Müller, Munich, 1992.

— *Das deutsche Vermögen in Polen. Ein Rechtsgutachten, Munich, 1996.*

Filip, Ota: Die stillen Toten unterm Klee — Wiedersehen mit Böhmen, Langen Müller, Munich, 1992.

— *Doch die Märchen sprechen deutsch. Geschichte aus Böhmen, Langen Müller, Munich, 1996.*

Foreign Relations of the United States: The Conferences at Malta and Yalta, 1945.

— *The Conference at Berlin, Bd. 1 und 2, 1945.*

— *1945, Bd. 2, General, Political and Economic Matters, Washington D.C.*

Frantzioch, Marion: Die Vertriebenen, Berlin, 1987.

Glotz, Peter: Die Vertreibung. Böhmen als Lehrstück, Berlin, 2003.

Göttinger Arbeitskreis (ed.): Documents of Humanity, Würzburg, 1961.

Gollancz, Victor: Our Threatened Values, Victor Gollancz Ltd, London, 1946

— *In Darkest Germany, Victor Gollancz Ltd, London, 1947*

Gornig, Gilbert: Das nördliche Ostpreußen gestern und heute. Bonn, 1995.

Grass, Günther: Crabwalk, Harcourt, New York, 2003.

Habel, Fritz Peter: Dokumente zur Sudetenfrage, 5. erw. Ausgabe, Munich, 2003.

Hartenstein, Michael: Die Geschichte der Oder-Neiße-Linie, 2. Aufl., Munich, 2007.

Haus der Geschichte der Bundesrepublik Deutschland (Hrsg.): Flucht, Vertreibung, Integration, 3rd edition, Bonn, 2006.

Helfert, Erich: Valley of the Shadow, Creative Arts Book Company, Berkeley, 1997.

Hillgruber, Andreas: Zweierlei Untergang, Siedler Verlag, Berlin, 1986.

Hirsch, Helga: Schweres Gepäck. Flucht und Vertreibung als Lebensthema. Hamburg, 2004.

House of Representatives, Committee on the Judiciary, Report No. 1841. 81st Congress, 2nd Session: "Expellees and Refugees of German Ethnic Origin", better known as "Walter Report", March 1950, Washington, D.C.

International Committee of the Red Cross: Report of the International Committee of the Red Cross on its Activities During the Second World War, Vols. 1–3, Geneva, 1948.

— *Report of the Joint Relief Commission 1941–46, Geneva, 1948.*

Jaksch, Wenzel: Europas Weg nach Potsdam, Munich 1990, Epilogue by Willy Brandt.

Kaps, Johannes: The Tragedy of Silesia. Munich, 1952.

Kennan, George F.: Memoirs, Vols. 1–2, Boston, 1967, 1972.

Kimminich, Otto: Das Recht auf die Heimat, 3rd edition, Bonn, 1989.

— *Die Menschenrechte in der Friedensregelung nach dem Zweiten Weltkrieg, Berlin, 1990.*

Kittel, Manfred: Vertreibung der Vertriebenen?, Munich, 2007.

Klein, Eckart: Diplomatischer Schutz im Hinblick auf Konfiskationen deutschen Vermögens durch Polen, Bonn, 1992.

— *Gutachten zur Rechtslage des im heutigem Polen entzogenen Privateigentums Deutscher, Potsdam, 2005.*

Koehler, Eve: Seven Susannahs: Daughters of the Danube. Milwaukee, 1977.

Kohout, Pavel: Sternstunde der Mörder, Prag, 1995, German version, Munich, 1996.

Kopelev, Lev: No Jail for Thought. London, 1976.

Koschyk, Hartmut (ed.): Das Recht auf die Heimat, Munich, 1992.

Kossert, Andreas: Kalte Heimat, Siedler Verlag, Munich, 2008.

Krutein, Eva: Eva's War. A True Story of Survival, Amador Publishers, Albuquerque New Mexico, 1990.

Lehndorff, Hans von: East Prussian Diary 1945–1947, London, 1979.

Lemberg, Hans und K. Erik Franzen: Die Vertriebenen. Berlin, 2001.

Lohne, Raymond: The Great Chicago Refugee Rescue, Picton Press, Rockland, Maine, 1997.

Luža, Radomír: The Transfer of the Sudeten Germans. New York, 1964.

MacDonogh, Giles: After the Reich. John Murray Publishers, London, 2007

Masaryk, Thomas: The Making of a State. London, 1927.

— *The Slavs among the Nations. London, 1916.*

Möller, Jakob Th. and Alfred de Zayas: United Nations Human Rights Committee Case Law: A Handbook, N.P. Engel Publishers, Kehl and Strassburg, 2009.

Naimark, Norman: The Russians in Germany, Harvard University Press, Cambridge, Massachusetts, 1995.

— *Fires of Hatred, Harvard Universtiy Press, Cambridge, Massachusetts, 2002.*

Neary, Brigitte and Holle Schneider-Ricks (eds.): Voices of Loss and Courage. German Women Recount their Expulsion from East Central Europe, Picton Press, Rockland, Maine, 2002.

Neitmann, Klaus: Die Staatsverträge des Deutschen Ordens in Preußen, Cologne, 1986.

Nitsch, Gunter: Weeds like Us, Author House, Bloomington Indiana, 2006

—   *Eine lange Flucht aus Ostpreußen, Ellert & Richter Verlag, 2011.*

Permanent Court of International Justice, Decisions and Judgments, Series A,B, The Hague 1919–1939.

Prinz, Friedrich: Geschichte Böhmens, Munich, 2003.

—   *Nation und Heimat, Munich, 2003.*

Rauschning, Hermann: Die Entdeutschung Posens and Westpreußens. Berlin, 1930.

Reichling, Gerhard: Die deutschen Vertriebenen in Zahlen, Teil 1/2, Bonn, 1986/89.

Řipka, Hubert: The Future of the Czechoslovak Germans, London, 1939.

—   *Munich. Before and After. London, 1939.*

Sack, John: An Eye for an Eye. Basic Books, New York, 1993.

Schimitzek, Stanislav. Truth or Conjecture: German Civilian Losses in the East, Warsaw, 1966.

Solzhenitsyn, Aleksandr: The Gulag Archipelago, New York, 1974.

—   *Prussian Nights: A Poem. Translated by Robert Conquest, New York, 1977.*

Staněk, Tomáš: Perzekuce 1945, Prague, 1996.

Statistisches Bundesamt: Die deutschen Vertreibungsverluste, Wiesbaden, 1958.

Steigerwald, Jacob: Profile of an American Danube Swabian ethnically cleansed under Tito, Translation and Interpretation Service, Littleton, Colorado, 2001.

Steinbach, Erika: Die Macht der Erinnerung, Universitas, Munich, 2010.

Stickler, Matthias: Ostdeutsch heißt Gesamtdeutsch, Düsseldorf, 2004.

Stiftung Zentrum gegen Vertreibungen: Erzwungene Wege — Flucht und Vertreibung im Europa des 20. Jahrhunderts, Wiesbaden, 2006.

Stump, Karl: The German-Russians: Two Centuries of Pioneering. Bonn, 1967.

Tannehill, Evelyne: Abandoned and forgotten. An Orphan Girl's Tale of Survival during World War II, Wheatmark, Tucson, Arizona, 2006.

Thornberry, Patrick: International Law and the Rights of Minorities, Oxford, 1991.

Urban, Thomas: Der Verlust. Die Vertreibung der Deutschen und Polen im 20. Jahrhundert, Munich, 2004.

Vardy, Stephen, Tooley Hunt (eds.): Ethnic Cleansing in Twentieth Century Europe, Columbia University Press, New York, 2003.

Wagner, Wolfgang: The Genesis of the Oder Neisse Line, Stuttgart, 1957.

Walter, Elizabeth: Barefoot in the Rubble, Pannonia Press, Palatine, Illinois, 1998.

Wiewiora, Boleslaw: *The Polish-German Frontier, Posen (Poznan), 1964.*

de Zayas, Alfred: *A Terrible Revenge, Palgrave/Macmillan, New York, 2006*

—   *Nemesis at Potsdam, Picton Press, Rockland, Maine, 2003.*

—   *Heimatrecht ist Menschenrecht, Universitas, Munich, 2001.*

—   *'Population Expulsion and Transfer', in: Rudolf Bernhard (ed.), Encyclopedia of Public International Law, Vol. 3, Amsterdam, 1997, pp. 1062–1068.*

—   *'Forced Population Transfer' in: Rüdiger Wolfrum (ed), Max Planck Encyclopedia of Public International Law, Oxford University Press, 2009.*

—   *'Curzon Line', 'Marshall Plan', 'Repatriation', in: Wolfrum (ed), Max Planck Encyclopedia of Public International Law, Oxford, 2010.*

—   *'The Right to the Homeland, Ethnic Cleansing and the International Criminal Tribunal for the Former Yugoslavia', in: Criminal Law Forum, Vol. 6, 1995, pp. 257–314.*

—   *'Minority Rights in the New Millennium', in: Geneva Post Quarterly, 2007, Vol. 2, pp. 155–208.*

—   *'International Law and Mass Population Transfers', in: Harvard International Law Journal, Vol. 16, 1975, pp. 207–258.*

—   *Collective expulsions: Norms, Jurisprudence, Remedies', in: Refugee Survey Quarterly, volume 16, 1997, pp. 149 et seq.*

Picture Credits

Cover: Ullstein Bild – pp. 3, 41, 47: Alfred de Zayas – p. 20-21: Drawn in the Department of State, Division of Geography and Cartography, January 10, 1945 / German Series, Map. 68 – p. 35: U.S. Army Signal Corps – p. 53: José Cruz/Abr (Oct 5, 1997) – p. 54: Fabio Pozzebom/Abr (May 10, 2007) – p. 59: Bundesarchiv – p. 61: Bund der Vertriebenen, Bonn – p. 62-64: Public Record Office, London, Document FO 371/46811 – p. 65 above: National Archives, Washington D.C. – pp. 65 below and 66 below: Sudetendeutsches Archiv, Munich – p. 66 above: TK Fotoservice – p. 72 above: B. Franken – p. 72 below: Michael Postmann.

German Speaking Areas in Europe in 1910...

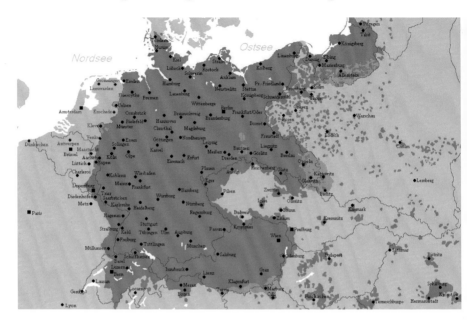

...and after the Expulsion, in 1950.

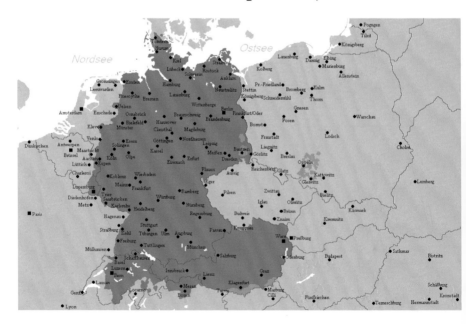